Commodore 64
Computer Programs
for Beginners

Books by Howard Adler
Commodore 64/VIC-20 Computer Programs for Beginners
101 Programming Tips & Tricks for the Commodore 64 &
  VIC-20
34 VIC-20 & Commodore 64 Computer Programs for Home,
  School & Office
Commodore 64 and VIC-20 Computer Program Writing
  Workbook

Commodore 64
Computer Programs
for Beginners

by Howard Adler

ARCsoft Publishers
WOODSBORO, MARYLAND

FIRST EDITION
FIRST PRINTING

© 1984 by ARCsoft Publishers, P.O. Box 132, Woodsboro, MD 21798 USA

ISBN 0-86668-033-0

Preface

The microcomputers from Commodore Business Machines Inc. are among the most popular around the world for use in the home, in the classroom, in the business office.   In fact, they may be the all-time best selling personal computers to date.

The lightweight desktop design of the ultramodern Model 64 and VIC and their powerful BASIC language capabilities place them in the forefront of the new wave of computers for hobbyists, students, teachers, parents, professionals and business persons who want to learn the new technology.

These powerful microcomputers are not toys! Their hardware and software combinations make them highly useful tools in the business environment and the classroom as well as in the home.

The total number of applications to which the various Commodore models can be put is limited only by the scope of the imagination. In this book, we have attempted to create and share 40 new practical sets of program ideas and appropriate applications software for your use.

This book, as well as all published by *ARCsoft Publishers,* is written for newcomers, novices and first-timers, as well as for advanced users of microcomputers. Our intention has been to provide easy-to-type-and-run programs for the Commodore 64 , VIC-20 and other computers using the Commodore version of the BASIC programming language. You type these programs into your computer and it does the rest. You do not have to be a programmer or program writer to use this book.

This volume is a companion to *101 Programming Tips & Tricks for the Commodore 64 and VIC-20* and to *34 VIC-20 & Commodore 64 Computer Programs for Home, School & Office* and to *Commodore 64 and VIC-20 Computer Program Writing Workbook.*

—Howard Adler

Table of Contents

Introduction

This is a book of programming advice and actual working programs for the Commodore Model 64, Commodore VIC-20, and other personal microcomputers using the Commodore Business Machines Inc. version of the BASIC programming language.

There continues to be a great need for practical and useful software for the new generation of popular personal computers. The Commodore 64, Commodore VIC-20, and other personal microcomputers from Commodore Business Machines Inc., are among the world's most popular computers for use in the home, in the classroom and even in the business office.

Commodore computers are powerful, versatile and flexible—but what can they do?

Once you've purchased the hardware, you need down-to-earth workable programs to run the computer. In this book, we provide 40 program ideas and appropriate complete easy-to-type ready-to-run sets of program listings for you to use in your own Commodore computer, to make your computer work for you.

These programs are useful in themselves. They also make good starting points for further development as you learn more and more about how to program your own computer. Read these programs. Type them into your computer. Watch them run. Analyze how the lines in the listings cause the computer to step through a sequence of operations to reach a final goal. You'll see how programs are organized, how they work. You can use these fun and practical programs and then, later, modify them to do more or different work. Expand them to suit your needs as your interests grow.

These programs are designed to be typed into your Commodore computer, just as you find them in this book, via the typewriter-style keyboard. No other programming is needed.

We assume you have read the owner's manual and instructional pamphlets which came with your Commodore computer and any accessories you may have. You know how to hook the computer to your TV and to other accessories you have. You know how to type programs into the computer. If you don't know these beginning steps, please review the instructions in the Commodore owner's manual.

You *do not have to be a programmer* to use these pieces of software. Just type them in, as you find them here, and run them. They will work!

Computer printouts

To make sure no errors appear in this book, we have written and tested each of these programs on our own Commodore computer and we have printed them on our VIC-1525E graphic printer. Some tests were made on the Commodore 64 and some on the VIC-20. The hardcopy printout from the 1525E line printer is reproduced directly in this book. Since no PEEK or POKE commands appear here, all of these programs work equally well on both the Commodore 64 and the VIC-20.

The Commodore computer operated the printer and listed these programs. No human hands came between the computer and these listings so no re-typing or proofreading errors have been introduced. You should find that these programs will run exactly as reproduced here.

If, after typing in a program, you get an error message from your Commodore computer, compare your typed program carefully with the program lines in this book. Remember that every space, punctuation mark, letter, number and symbol counts and must be in the computer exactly as in this book.

If you do get such an error message, the most likely cause will be found to have been a typing error in transferring the program from this book into the computer. However, should you find an error in this book, please call it to the attention of the author by sending a postcard or letter to him in care of *ARCsoft Publishers,* P.O. Box 132, Woodsboro, MD 21798 USA. The author will appreciate being able to make any necessary corrections to future editions of this book.

Commodore 64/VIC-20 compatibility

Most programs written on the Commodore 64, in BASIC, will run on the Commodore model VIC-20. Similarly, most VIC-20 BASIC programs will run on the Commodore 64.

However, programs using the BASIC commands *PEEK* and *POKE* are not interchangeable between the two computer models from Commodore. The BASIC word POKE sends data into a specific memory location in the computer. Such a memory location is identified by a number, often called the *memory POKE number.* The various memory location numbers in the Commodore 64 are different from those in the VIC-20. Thus, a POKE command which works in the Commodore 64 won't work in the VIC-20. And a POKE which works in VIC-20 memory won't work in the Commodore 64. Please refer to the owner's manual which was supplied by Commodore with your computer to determine the exact memory POKE numbers for your computer.

PEEK, on the other hand, allows you to examine the contents of specific memory locations within the computer. You can PEEK into a memory location to see what already has been POKEd there. VIC-20 programs using PEEK will not find the same memory location numbers on the Commodore 64, and model 64 programs will not find the same

PEEK locations in the VIC-20. Thus, PEEK will not work interchangeably between the two programs.

We have attempted to eliminate all PEEK and POKE uses from the programs in this book so you will not have to worry about the compatibility problem.

How to use this book

This book has been organized into four sections for your convenience in finding programs. The first section includes programs of a money or financial nature.

The second section includes programs which we hope you will find fun to use. Some are games, some are practical and some can be used to wow your friends by demonstrating the seemingly-mysterious ways in which the computer can operate faster than a speeding bullet.

The third section holds programs designed to be educational in nature. Using these can provide fun and excitement while learning occurs.

The fourth section finds the computer making life easier by doing the hard math which can be very practical yet difficult to perform. These turn your Commodore computer into a super-fast electronic helper!

Naturally, these sections as we have divided the book are not rigid or exclusive. You undoubtedly will find something in the math or finance or fun area which will be educational. The educational programs can be fun and practical.

Try them all. They are great fun to run. And they are especially designed to be short so you won't have to spend hours typing any one program into your Commodore computer.

Please note that each and every one of the programs in this book is complete and ready-to-run in BASIC for you to use. Try them all. They are great fun to run. They are especially designed to be short so you won't have to spend hours typing in one program.

As your knowledge of BASIC and how it makes your Commodore computer work grows, you will be able to build on these elementary programs to create ever-more-complex schemes for practical applications.

Endless running

Many of the programs in this book will continue to run until you command them off manually via the RUN STOP key. You may stop any run, at any time, by pressing the RUN STOP key on the left side of the keyboard. This RUN STOP function in the Commodore computers is the same as what is called BREAK on other microcomputers.

REMarks

As you read through the 40 programs in this book, you will notice very few REM, or remarks, statements. The author's training in writing BASIC-language computer programs included an emphasis on brevity and saving memory space. A sharp editing pencil was in order—and still is!

REMarks and explanations in software are out. Honing, fine tuning and waste trimming are in. Use of coding form program-writing worksheets is encouraged. Such worksheets can be found in the publication, *Commodore Computer Program Writing Workbook,* available from ARCsoft Publishers. Your objective always should be to make the most efficient use of available memory.

Here's another important note to remember: even though they may be headed toward the same goal, no two programmers will write the exact same list of BASIC instructions, or program lines, from scratch. As you load these programs into your Commodore computer, one at a time, you'll make modifications to suit your personal needs and interests if you want to. For instance, the exact wording of PRINT statements can be changed. Or two or more programs can be combined into one grand scheme. Your applications may vary.

By the way, if you want to load more than one of these programs into your computer at the same time, be sure to use different sets of line numbers for different programs. For example, only one line can be numbered 10. There cannot be two lines numbered 10 in the computer at the same time.

We use the words ENTER and RETURN interchangeably. Programmers today generally mix the use of the two words, to mean the same thing. In this case, we mean the RETURN key on the right hand side of the Commodore keyboard. For example, you ENTER a line into program memory by typing it into the computer and pressing the RETURN key at the end of the line. Pressing RETURN causes it to be ENTERed into the computer's program memory.

Other computers

These programs will run on other computers which use the BASIC language. However, to run these programs on other non-Commodore computers, you probably will have to make at least slight modifications to program lines. Graphics commands, especially, will differ elsewhere. Also, use of multiple-statement lines, using the colon (:), can be quite different in other brand-names of computer hardware.

Also, if you use a non-Commodore computer, such things as line numbering, spacing, logical tests, multiplication symbols, print statements and other instructions may be different.

Refer to the owner's manual which came with your non-Commodore computer. Compare its version of the BASIC language with Commodore BASIC.

The author would like to have your suggestions for future editions of this work, or for other titles in this series for the Commodore computers. The author may be addressed in care of *ARCsoft Publishers.*

Standalone vs. subroutine

The programs in this book may be used as portions of larger lists of instructions to your Commodore computer. They can be written in as GOTO or GOSUB objects. To do so, make appropriate changes to the first line (usually numbered 10 in this book) and to the last line of each program.

If you create a subroutine, remember that every GOSUB must have a RETURN. RETURN must be the last line of every subroutine.

If you work one of these programs into a larger set of instructions, be especially careful of your memory (variable) names or labels. They must agree with, and fit into, those you are using in the main program. Also, be careful of line numbers. No two programs can occupy the exact same set of line numbers.

Learning programming

These programs are written to be typed into your Commodore computer just as you find them here—with no extra programming needed. We assume you know how to turn on your computer and how to go about typing in a program.

Many of the programs and most of the programming advice in this book will be of interest to old hands, as well as newcomers, since we are presenting new twists and more powerful exercises aimed at making your computer do more work, more quickly.

Amidst the three dozen programs in this book, you will find countless ideas for using your computer. Each piece of software is intended to make you a more-versatile programmer and make your programming chores lighter.

This is not a replacement for the owner's manual which came with your Commodore computer. You need to read it thoroughly, first, then use this book as a supplement.

Use this book to stimulate your thinking about how to approach various software problems and projects. Use it to get good ideas for new and different approaches to all of your programming goals. As you grow and develop as a program author, modify these programs to make your computer do even more.

Happy programming!

Home Finance Programs

Car Payments

Shopping for a new car?   Use your computer
to compute quickly the potential monthly car payment
on various models.

Imagine you want an $8000 car and are prepared to put
up $1000 against the purchase. You want to arrange to
finance the car for 36 months. You know the current annual
interest rate on car loans is 15 percent.

Key in those few numbers and the computer instantly
tells you the car payment will be $242.66 per month.

Program Listing

```
10 PRINT CHR$(147):REM CLEAR SCREEN
20 GOSUB 300
30 PRINT"AUTOMOBILE PAYMENT"
40 GOSUB 300
50 PRINT
60 PRINT"PURCHASE PRICE $"
70 INPUT T
80 PRINT"DOWN PAYMENT $"
90 INPUT R
100 PRINT"NUMBER OF MONTHS"
110 INPUT N
120 PRINT"ANNUAL INTEREST %"
130 INPUT I
140 I=(0.01*I)/12
150 P=(T-R)*I/(1-1/(1+I)↑N)
160 PP=INT(100*P+0.5)/100
170 PRINT
180 PRINT"PAYMENT $",PP
190 PRINT
200 GOSUB 300
210 PRINT
220 INPUT"FOR MORE PRESS RETURN";K$
230 CLR
240 GOTO 10
300 FOR L=1 TO 22
310 PRINT CHR$(115);
320 NEXT L
330 RETURN
```

Sample Run

❀❀❀❀❀❀❀❀❀❀❀❀❀❀❀❀❀❀❀❀❀
AUTOMOBILE PAYMENT
❀❀❀❀❀❀❀❀❀❀❀❀❀❀❀❀❀❀❀❀❀

PURCHASE PRICE $
 8000
DOWN PAYMENT $
 1000
NUMBER OF MONTHS
 36
ANNUAL INTEREST %
 15

PAYMENT $ 242.66

❀❀❀❀❀❀❀❀❀❀❀❀❀❀❀❀❀❀❀❀❀

FOR MORE PRESS RETURN

Money Grows

This program shows you how your money grows when deposited in a savings account at a certain annual interest rate, compounded monthly.

The program will have the computer ask for the initial amount of principal saved by depositing in the account. Then the annual interest rate and the number of months to be displayed. The result of the run is a display of the changing principal as months pass and interest is added on.

Line 10 clears the text screen. Lines 20 to 40 take in data from you. Lines 50 to 90 put out the results. Very handy!

Line 85 is a timing loop to slow down the presentation so you can digest the information. To make it even slower, increase the number 400 in line 85. To make it faster, decrease the number 400 in line 85.

Program Listing

```
10 PRINT CHR$(147):REM CLEAR SCREEN
20 INPUT"PRINCIPAL $";P
30 INPUT"ANNUAL INTEREST %";R
40 INPUT"NUMBER MONTHS";M
45 PRINT CHR$(147):REM CLEAR SCREEN
50 PRINT"MONTH";SPC(7);"BALANCE"
55 FOR Q=1 TO M
60 I=(P*(0.01*R))/12
70 P=P+I
75 PP=INT(100*P+0.5)/100
80 PRINT Q,PP
85 FOR T=1 TO 400:NEXT T
90 NEXT Q
100 PRINT:PRINT
110 INPUT"FOR MORE PRESS RETURN";K$
120 CLR:GOTO 10
```

Sample Run

```
PRINCIPAL $ 1000
ANNUAL INTEREST % 10
NUMBER MONTHS 12
MONTH         BALANCE
  1            1008.33
  2            1016.74
  3            1025.21
  4            1033.75
  5            1042.37
  6            1051.05
  7            1059.81
  8            1068.64
  9            1077.55
 10            1086.53
 11            1095.58
 12            1104.71

FOR MORE PRESS RETURN
```

21

Monthly Loan Payment

Here's a fast computation of the monthly payment on a loan. The amount borrowed, the principle, is stored in memory location P. I is the annual interest rate and N is the number of payments. I is converted to a monthly interest rate and then to a decimal in line 50.

Program Listing

```
10 PRINT CHR$(147):REM CLEAR SCREEN
20 PRINT"AMOUNT BORROWED $"
25 INPUT P
30 PRINT"ANNUAL INTEREST %"
35 INPUT I
40 PRINT"NUMBER OF PAYMENTS"
45 INPUT N
50 I=0.01*(I/12)
60 M=(P*I)/(1-((1+I)↑(-N)))
70 PRINT:PRINT
80 PRINT"MONTHLY PAYMENT IS","$";M
90 PRINT:PRINT:PRINT
100 PRINT"TO DO ANOTHER,"
110 INPUT"PRESS RETURN";K$
120 CLR
130 GOTO 10
```

Sample Run

```
AMOUNT BORROWED $ 2000
ANNUAL INTEREST %  8
NUMBER OF PAYMENTS  36

MONTHLY PAYMENT IS $ 62.6727286


AMOUNT BORROWED $ 1000
ANNUAL INTEREST %  14
NUMBER OF PAYMENTS  48

MONTHLY PAYMENT IS $ 27.3264763
```

Unit Price

Suppose you find 895 green Widgets and buy them for $695. How much did each green Widget cost? Rounded off, 78 cents.

Unit price is total price divided by quantity. The quantity can be expressed in weight, total numbers, etc. It works the same whether you are talking about pounds of coffee, yards of concrete, gallons of ice cream, boxes of books, or units of Widgets.

This program asks for the name of the item, quantity purchased and total price paid. It then displays quantity, name, total and unit price.

Program Listing

```
10 PRINT CHR$(147)
20 PRINT"ITEM NAME:"
25 INPUT N$
30 PRINT
35 PRINT"QUANTITY OF ITEMS:"
40 INPUT Q
45 PRINT
50 PRINT"TOTAL PRICE"
55 PRINT"PAID FOR ITEMS:"
60 INPUT"$ ";P
70 U=P/Q
80 UU=INT(100*U+0.5)/100
90 PRINT
100 PRINT N$;" UNIT PRICE"
110 PRINT"IS $";UU
120 PRINT:PRINT:PRINT
130 INPUT"FOR MORE PRESS RETURN";K$
140 CLR:GOTO 10
```

Sample Run

```
ITEM NAME:
WIDGET
```

```
QUANTITY OF ITEMS:
 999

TOTAL PRICE
PAID FOR ITEMS:
$  14653

WIDGET UNIT PRICE
IS $ 14.67


FOR MORE PRESS RETURN

ITEM NAME:
THINGAMABOB

QUANTITY OF ITEMS:
 895

TOTAL PRICE
PAID FOR ITEMS:
$   695

THINGAMABOB UNIT PRICE
IS $ .78


FOR MORE PRESS RETURN
```

Shopper's Friend

This program finds the computer asking for certain information and then telling you which product brand name is the best buy.

The computer wil ask for the brand name of a product, the quantity in the product package, and the price of the package. Then it will ask for the name, quantity and price for a second product.

After digesting all this information, it will tell you the brand name of the best-buy product and show you the unit prices for both brand names so you can agree with the computer's judgment.

For example, suppose you were looking at corn flakes in boxes, one by Post and one by Kellogg. Suppose the Post box contained 24 ounces of flakes and was priced on the grocery shelf at $1.98 while the Kellogg box held 18 ounces and was priced at $1.59. Which would be the better buy based on unit price per ounce of flakes?

Run the data through your computer and you'll find it computes the Post corn flakes to be the best buy with a unit price of 8¢ vs. the Kellogg unit price of 9¢.

By the way, if the unit prices turn out to be equal, the computer will say they are equal.

Program Listing

```
10 PRINT CHR$(147):REM CLEAR SCREEN
20 PRINT SPC(3);"SHOPPER'S FRIEND"
30 FOR L=1 TO 22:PRINT"*";:NEXT L:PRINT
40 INPUT"FIRST BRAND";X$
50 INPUT"QUANTITY";M
55 IF M=0 THEN 50
60 INPUT"PRICE";N
70 INPUT"SECOND BRAND";Y$
80 INPUT"QUANTITY";Q
85 IF Q=0 THEN 80
90 INPUT"PRICE";R
100 PRINT CHR$(147):REM CLEAR SCREEN
110 IF N/M=R/Q THEN 500
120 IF N/M<R/Q THEN 300
200 PRINT Y$;" IS BEST BUY"
210 GOTO 400
300 PRINT X$;" IS BEST BUY"
400 PRINT
410 PRINT X$;" UNIT=$";INT(100*(N/M)
    +0.5)/100
420 PRINT Y$;" UNIT=$";INT(100*(R/Q)
    +0.5)/100
```

```
430 FOR L=1 TO 8:PRINT:NEXT L
440 INPUT"FOR MORE PRESS RETURN";K$
450 CLR
460 GOTO 10
500 PRINT
510 PRINT X$;" = ";Y$
520 GOTO 400
```

Selling Prices
Of World Currencies

Your own world currency guide allows you to convert money from one currency to another quickly.

The conversion amounts built into program lines 100 to 590 were selected from the New York City market one day in August 1982. You should check later lists of selling prices and modify the DATA lines (program lines 100 to 590) to show the current, correct amount. Check your local bank or stock broker for the latest exchange rates.

The program will hold even more currencies, if you need them, even in the minimum no-extra-memory-added computer. Of course, you could gain even more bytes of program memory for other use if you used abbreviations for country names or currency names. The problem with such abbreviations is that you have to remember them later!

As written here, the program includes 50 countries. If you change the total number of countries by changing the DATA lines, be sure to change the number 50 in line 630. The program will run endlessly until you press STOP to end it.

Program Listing

```
10 PRINT CHR$(147):REM CLEAR SCREEN
100 DATA ARGENTINA,PESO,.0001
110 DATA AUSTRALIA,DOLLAR,.9815
120 DATA AUSTRIA,SCHILLING,.0584
130 DATA BAHAMAS,DOLLAR,1
```

```
140 DATA BELGIUM,FRANC,.0215
150 DATA BELIZE,DOLLAR,.5
160 DATA BERMUDA,DOLLAR,1
170 DATA BRAZIL,CRUZEIRO,.0053
180 DATA CANADA,DOLLAR,.8114
190 DATA CHILE,PESO,.0256
200 DATA CHINA,YUAN,.5236
210 DATA COLOMBIA,PESO,.0256
220 DATA CYPRUS,POUND,2.1552
230 DATA DENMARK,KRONE,.1178
240 DATA ECUADOR,SUCRE,.0303
250 DATA EGYPT,POUND,1.2195
260 DATA FINLAND,MARKKA,.2129
270 DATA FRANCE,FRANC,.1475
280 DATA GERMANY,MARK,.4137
290 DATA GREAT BRITAIN,POUND,1.776
300 DATA GREECE,DRACHMA,.0146
310 DATA HAITI,GOURDE,.2
320 DATA HONG KONG,DOLLAR,.1682
330 DATA HUNGARY,FORINT,.029
340 DATA ICELAND,KRONA,.0994
350 DATA INDIA,RUPEE,.1053
360 DATA IRAQ,DINAR,3.3862
370 DATA IRELAND,POUND,1.4155
380 DATA ISRAEL,SHEKEL,.0377
390 DATA ITALY,LIRA,.0008
400 DATA JAPAN,YEN,.004
410 DATA MEXICO,PESO,.0111
420 DATA NETHERLANDS,GUILDER,.3781
430 DATA NEW ZEALAND,DOLLAR,.7405
440 DATA NIGERIA,NAIRA,1.4808
450 DATA NORWAY,KRONE,.1523
460 DATA PAKISTAN,RUPEE,.0809
470 DATA PERU,SOL,.0014
480 DATA POLAND,ZLOTY,.0125
490 DATA PORTUGAL,ESCUDO,.0118
500 DATA SAUDI ARABIA,RIYAL,.2907
510 DATA SOUTH AFRICA,RAND,.8607
520 DATA SPAIN,PESETA,.0091
530 DATA SWEDEN,KRONA,.1653
540 DATA SWITZERLAND,FRANC,.4902
550 DATA THAILAND,BAHT,.0435
```

```
560 DATA TURKEY,LIRA,.0066
570 DATA USSR,RUBLE,1.3986
580 DATA VENEZUELA,BOLIVAR,.2329
590 DATA ZAMBIA,KWACHA,1.084
600 PRINT"COUNTRY:"
610 INPUT C$
620 PRINT
630 FOR L=1 TO 50
640 READ CC$
650 READ M$
660 READ V
670 IF CC$=C$ THEN 720
680 CC$=""
690 NEXT L
700 RESTORE
710 GOTO 600
720 RESTORE
730 PRINT M$;"=US$ X";V
740 PRINT:PRINT
750 PRINT"DO YOU WISH TO"
760 PRINT"CONVERT DOLLARS"
770 PRINT"TO ";M$
780 PRINT"PRESS Y(YES) OR N(NO)"
790 GET K$
800 IF K$="" THEN 790
810 IF K$="Y" THEN 900
820 IF K$="N" THEN 840
830 GOTO 780
840 FOR Z=1 TO 12:PRINT:NEXT Z
850 CLR
860 GOTO 600
900 PRINT CHR$(147)
910 PRINT"DOLLAR AMOUNT"
920 INPUT"TO BE CONVERTED: ";D
930 CD=D*V
940 PRINT
950 PRINT D;C$;" ";M$
960 PRINT TAB(1) "US$";CD
970 GOTO 840
```

Sample Run

```
COUNTRY:
```

ZAMBIA

KWACHA=US$ X 1.084

DO YOU WISH TO
CONVERT DOLLARS
TO KWACHA
PRESS Y(YES) OR N(NO)
Y

DOLLAR AMOUNT
 123

 123 ZAMBIA KWACHA
US$ 133.332

COUNTRY:
BELIZE

DOLLAR=US$ X .5

DO YOU WISH TO
CONVERT DOLLARS
TO DOLLAR
PRESS Y(YES) OR N(NO)
N

COUNTRY:
HAITI

GOURDE=US$ X .2

DO YOU WISH TO
CONVERT DOLLARS
TO GOURDE
PRESS Y(YES) OR N(NO)
Y

DOLLAR AMOUNT
 77

77 HAITI GOURDE
US$ 15.4

COUNTRY:
FINLAND

MARKKA=US$ X .2129

DO YOU WISH TO
CONVERT DOLLARS
TO MARKKA
PRESS Y(YES) OR N(NO)
N

COUNTRY:
CYPRUS

POUND=US$ X 2.1552

DO YOU WISH TO
CONVERT DOLLARS
TO POUND
PRESS Y(YES) OR N(NO)
Y

DOLLAR AMOUNT
 54321

 54321 CYPRUS POUND
US$ 117072.619

Fun Programs

Code Groups

Need some secret codes for your latest sensitive mission? How about sets of five random letters for use in Morse code practice?

This program has the computer generate an endless string of random combinations of five letters.

Program Listing

```
10 PRINT CHR$(147):REM SCREEN CLEAR
20 FOR L=1 TO 5
30 N=INT(91*RND(1))
40 IF N<65 THEN 30
50 PRINT CHR$(N);
60 NEXT L
70 PRINT:GOTO 20
```

Sample Run

```
JXSRV
SXYKR
NAEHB
TQVSM
RPVKQ
AWLZV
ZNAWP
YTDMJ
RKEZK

BMLHJ
USGOO
YRSKS
HTSKQ
UDVUN
RSUHF
ICHVI
IMLFE
BYWHN

QSYRI
NLLML
```

```
VZQOR
UFAPA
YNBNR
TDWSO
NPGGH
VEMFT
GULFD
```

Program Listing

```
1 REM******THIS PROGRAM LISTING HAS THE
2 REM******COMPUTER PRINT ON A LINE PRINTER
3 REM******WHICH MUST BE CONNECTED TO THE
  COMPUTER
4 REM******TO USE THIS PROGRAM
5 REM**************************************
8 OPEN 3,4
9 CMD 3
10 PRINT CHR$(147):REM SCREEN CLEAR
20 FOR L=1 TO 5
30 N=INT(91*RND(1))
40 IF N<65 THEN 30
50 PRINT CHR$(N);
60 NEXT L
70 PRINT:GOTO 20
```

Sample Run

```
AIURR
ZNCBS
RGHRF
BTHLN
XQJRT
KLZZN
GDAES
VVYJK
MCTFR
FXYMY
```

Secret Message

Secret messages can be lots of fun! They often are composed of codes in which letters of the alphabet have been replaced by numbers.

In this easy-to-use program, the computer generates a list of pseudorandom numbers and assigns one number to each letter of the alphabet. You use the numbers, in lieu of letters, to write notes to your friends.

There is very little chance of the same number being assigned to two different letters because available numbers range from zero to 999.

When typing this program into your computer, be sure to separate the alphabet letters with commas in line 100.

By the way, note the nice two-column screen printing format! Line 250 does that.

Program Listing

```
10 PRINT CHR$(147):REM CLEAR SCREEN
20 Z=RND(-TI)
100 DATA A,B,C,D,E,F,G,H,I,J,K,L,M,N,
    O,P,Q,R,S,T,U,V,W,X,Y,Z
200 FOR N=1 TO 13
210 C=INT(1000*RND(1))
220 READ L$
230 D=INT(1000*RND(1))
240 READ J$
250 PRINT L$;" ";C,J$;" ";D
260 NEXT N
300 GET K$
310 IF K$="" THEN 300
320 RESTORE
330 GOTO 10
```

Sample Run

A	861	B	110
C	73	D	56
E	783	F	714
G	444	H	228

I	160	J	25
K	954	L	386
M	952	N	279
O	944	P	999
Q	869	R	310
S	323	T	401
U	603	V	9
W	286	X	534
Y	352	Z	33

Daily Code

Need to have a secret code each day of the year? This software generates a list of code numbers. Of course, you can change the list every day if you wish.

Program Listing

```
10 PRINT CHR$(147):Z=RND(-TI)
20 GOSUB 200
100 PRINT"SUNDAY",C:GOSUB 200
110 PRINT"MONDAY",C:GOSUB 200
120 PRINT"TUESDAY",C:GOSUB 200
130 PRINT"WEDNESDAY",C:GOSUB 200
140 PRINT"THURSDAY",C:GOSUB 200
150 PRINT"FRIDAY",C:GOSUB 200
160 PRINT"SATURDAY",C:END
200 C=INT(10000*RND(1))
210 IF C<1000 THEN 200
220 RETURN
```

Sample Run

```
SUNDAY        9722
MONDAY        1496
TUESDAY       7648
WEDNESDAY     1930
THURSDAY      5119
```

```
FRIDAY                    3417
SATURDAY                  2745

READY.


SUNDAY                    9329
MONDAY                    7304
TUESDAY                   5959
WEDNESDAY                 4127
THURSDAY                  8092
FRIDAY                    3932
SATURDAY                  7479


READY.


SUNDAY                    2720
MONDAY                    9647
TUESDAY                   7003
WEDNESDAY                 3859
THURSDAY                  4598
FRIDAY                    9484
SATURDAY                  2292


READY.
```

Chinese Zodiac

The most-famous oriental zodiac calendar is divided into twelve-year groups, each year having a different animal sign. The sign under which a person is born is believed to determine the circumstances of his life and the kind of person he is.

The animals are rat, ox, tiger, rabbit, dragon, snake, horse, sheep, monkey, cock, dog and boar.

Run this program. When asked by the computer, type in the year of your birth. The computer will find which animal sign corresponds to your birth year and present you with information concerning your own circumstances.

The computer names the animal, describes your personality traits, tells which other animal signs are compatible with your own, and tells which animal signs are your opposite.

This game goes on endlessly until you press the BREAK key to stop the run.

Program Listing

```
10 PRINT CHR$(147):REM SCREEN CLEAR
20 INPUT"YEAR OF BIRTH";Y$
30 X$=RIGHT$(Y$,2)
40 N=VAL(X$)
50 IF (N/12)=INT(N/12) THEN 200
60 IF ((N-1)/12)=INT((N-1)/12) THEN 250
70 IF ((N-2)/12)=INT((N-2)/12) THEN 300
80 IF ((N-3)/12)=INT((N-3)/12) THEN 350
90 IF ((N-4)/12)=INT((N-4)/12) THEN 400
100 IF ((N-5)/12)=INT((N-5)/12) THEN 450
110 IF ((N-6)/12)=INT((N-6)/12) THEN 500
120 IF ((N-7)/12)=INT((N-7)/12) THEN 550
130 IF ((N-8)/12)=INT((N-8)/12) THEN 600
140 IF ((N-9)/12)=INT((N-9)/12) THEN 650
150 IF ((N-10)/12)=INT((N-10)/12) THEN 700
160 IF ((N-11)/12)=INT((N-11)/12) THEN 750
170 GOTO 10
200 PRINT:PRINT Y$;" SIGN: RAT"
210 PRINT:PRINT"YOU ARE:"
215 PRINT"AMBITIOUS, SINCERE"
220 PRINT:PRINT"COMPATIBLE WITH:"
225 PRINT"DRAGON, MONKEY"
230 PRINT:PRINT"OPPOSITE OF:"
235 PRINT"HORSE"
240 GOTO 800
250 PRINT:PRINT Y$;" SIGN: OX"
260 PRINT:PRINT"YOU ARE:"
265 PRINT"LEADER, BRIGHT, CHEERY"
```

```
270 PRINT:PRINT"COMPATIBLE WITH:"
275 PRINT"SNAKE, COCK"
280 PRINT:PRINT"OPPOSITE OF:"
285 PRINT"SHEEP"
290 GOTO 800
300 PRINT:PRINT Y$;" SIGN: TIGER"
310 PRINT:PRINT"YOU ARE:"
315 PRINT"SENSITIVE, COURAGEOUS"
320 PRINT:PRINT"COMPATIBLE WITH:"
325 PRINT"HORSE, DOG"
330 PRINT:PRINT"OPPOSITE OF:"
335 PRINT"MONKEY"
340 GOTO 800
350 PRINT:PRINT Y$;" SIGN: RABBIT"
360 PRINT:PRINT"YOU ARE:"
365 PRINT"TALENTED, AFFECTIONATE"
370 PRINT:PRINT"COMPATIBLE WITH:"
375 PRINT"SHEEP, BOAR"
380 PRINT:PRINT"OPPOSITE OF:"
385 PRINT"COCK"
390 GOTO 800
400 PRINT:PRINT Y$;" SIGN: DRAGON"
410 PRINT:PRINT"YOU ARE:"
415 PRINT"ROBUST, PASSIONATE"
420 PRINT:PRINT"COMPATIBLE WITH:"
425 PRINT"MONKEY, RAT"
430 PRINT:PRINT"OPPOSITE OF:"
435 PRINT"DOG"
440 GOTO 800
450 PRINT:PRINT Y$;" SIGN: SNAKE"
460 PRINT:PRINT"YOU ARE:"
465 PRINT"WISE, INTENSE"
470 PRINT:PRINT"COMPATIBLE WITH:"
475 PRINT"OX, COCK"
480 PRINT:PRINT"OPPOSITE OF:"
485 PRINT"BOAR"
490 GOTO 800
500 PRINT:PRINT Y$;" SIGN: HORSE"
510 PRINT:PRINT"YOU ARE:"
515 PRINT"ATTRACTIVE, POPULAR"
520 PRINT:PRINT"COMPATIBLE WITH:"
525 PRINT"TIGER, DOG"
```

```
530 PRINT:PRINT"OPPOSITE OF:"
535 PRINT"RAT"
540 GOTO 800
550 PRINT:PRINT Y$;" SIGN: SHEEP"
560 PRINT:PRINT"YOU ARE:"
565 PRINT"STYLISH, PRIVATE"
570 PRINT:PRINT"COMPATIBLE WITH:"
575 PRINT"BOAR, RABBIT"
580 PRINT:PRINT"OPPOSITE OF:"
585 PRINT"OX"
590 GOTO 800
600 PRINT:PRINT Y$;" SIGN: MONKEY"
610 PRINT:PRINT"YOU ARE:"
615 PRINT"PERSUASIVE,INTELLIGENT"
620 PRINT:PRINT"COMPATIBLE WITH:"
625 PRINT"DRAGON, RAT"
630 PRINT:PRINT"OPPOSITE OF:"
635 PRINT"TIGER"
640 GOTO 800
650 PRINT:PRINT Y$;" SIGN: COCK"
660 PRINT:PRINT"YOU ARE:"
665 PRINT"PIONEERING,"
666 PRINT"SEEKING TRUTH"
670 PRINT:PRINT"COMPATIBLE WITH:"
675 PRINT"SNAKE, OX"
680 PRINT:PRINT"OPPOSITE OF:"
685 PRINT"RABBIT"
690 GOTO 800
700 PRINT:PRINT Y$;" SIGN: DOG"
710 PRINT:PRINT"YOU ARE:"
715 PRINT"GENEROUS, LOYAL"
720 PRINT:PRINT"COMPATIBLE WITH:"
725 PRINT"HORSE, TIGER"
730 PRINT:PRINT"OPPOSITE OF:"
735 PRINT"DRAGON"
740 GOTO 800
750 PRINT:PRINT Y$;" SIGN: BOAR"
760 PRINT:PRINT"YOU ARE:"
765 PRINT"GALLANT, NOBLE"
770 PRINT:PRINT"COMPATIBLE WITH:"
775 PRINT"RABBIT, SHEEP"
780 PRINT:PRINT"OPPOSITE OF:"
```

```
785 PRINT"SNAKE"
800 PRINT
810 PRINT"TO DO MORE,"
820 INPUT"PRESS RETURN";K$
830 GOTO 10
```

Guess The Number

Here it is! The world's oldest, longest running, most popular game: Guess The Number.

When you start the program running, the computer thinks of a number and stores that away. You try to guess the number. If your number is too high, the computer says, "TOO HIGH."

If you are too low, the computer will report "TOO LOW." The possible numbers range from zero to 100.

Program Listing

```
10 PRINT CHR$(147):Z=RND(-TI)
20 FOR L=1 TO 20:PRINT"*";:NEXT L:PRINT
30 N=INT(101*RND(1))
40 INPUT"GUESS THE NUMBER";G
50 IF G>N THEN PRINT"TOO HIGH":GOTO 40
60 IF G<N THEN PRINT"TOO LOW":GOTO 40
70 PRINT:PRINT"RIGHT !"
80 PRINT"LET'S GO AGAIN"
90 GOTO 20
```

Sample Run

```
********************
GUESS THE NUMBER 100
TOO HIGH
GUESS THE NUMBER 1
TOO LOW
GUESS THE NUMBER 33
TOO HIGH
```

```
GUESS THE NUMBER 9
TOO LOW
GUESS THE NUMBER 26
TOO HIGH
GUESS THE NUMBER 16
TOO HIGH
GUESS THE NUMBER 12
TOO LOW
GUESS THE NUMBER 13

RIGHT !
LET'S GO AGAIN
**********************
GUESS THE NUMBER 50
TOO LOW
GUESS THE NUMBER 75
TOO HIGH
GUESS THE NUMBER 67
TOO HIGH
GUESS THE NUMBER 53
TOO HIGH
GUESS THE NUMBER 52

RIGHT !
LET'S GO AGAIN
**********************
GUESS THE NUMBER 50
TOO HIGH
GUESS THE NUMBER 25
TOO HIGH
GUESS THE NUMBER 13
TOO LOW
GUESS THE NUMBER 20
TOO HIGH
GUESS THE NUMBER 17
TOO HIGH
GUESS THE NUMBER 15

RIGHT !
LET'S GO AGAIN
```

Original Hi/Lo Game

Here it is. Where everybody started in micro-computer programming back in the Seventies. The first game ever played was a high-low guess-the-number routine.

The computer selects a secret number. You try to guess it. The computer tells you whether or not you are too high, too low, or right on the number.

Here's how it works: the secret number can be zero to 1000. Line 100 generates a random number (the secret number) and stores it. Line 210 asks you to guess the number.

Lines 300-310 decide if you are right or wrong. Line 220 keeps track of the number of attempts.

Program Listing

```
10 PRINT CHR$(147):REM CLEAR SCREEN
20 Z=RND(-TI)
30 T=0
100 R=INT(1000*RND(1))
200 PRINT"I HAVE A SECRET NUMBER"
210 INPUT"CAN YOU GUESS IT";B
220 T=T+1
230 PRINT:PRINT:PRINT"THAT WAS TRY NO.";T
300 IF B>R THEN PRINT:INPUT"TOO HIGH,
    GUESS AGAIN";B:GOTO 220
310 IF B<R THEN PRINT:INPUT"TOO LOW,GUESS
    AGAIN";B:GOTO 220
400 PRINT CHR$(147)
410 PRINT"YES, YOU GOT IT"
420 PRINT R;"IS THE NUMBER"
430 PRINT"YOU GOT IT"
440 PRINT"IN";T;"TRIES"
450 FOR L=1 TO 10:PRINT:NEXT L
460 CLR
470 GOTO 30
```

Sample Run

```
I HAVE A SECRET NUMBER
CAN YOU GUESS IT 500
THAT WAS TRY NO. 1
TOO HIGH,GUESS AGAIN 250
THAT WAS TRY NO. 2
TOO LOW,GUESS AGAIN 400
THAT WAS TRY NO. 3
TOO HIGH,GUESS AGAIN 300
THAT WAS TRY NO. 4
TOO LOW,GUESS AGAIN 290
THAT WAS TRY NO. 5
TOO LOW,GUESS AGAIN 350
THAT WAS TRY NO. 6
TOO HIGH,GUESS AGAIN 340
THAT WAS TRY NO. 7
TOO HIGH,GUESS AGAIN 330
THAT WAS TRY NO. 8
TOO HIGH,GUESS AGAIN 320
THAT WAS TRY NO. 9
TOO LOW,GUESS AGAIN 310
THAT WAS TRY NO. 10
TOO LOW,GUESS AGAIN 325
THAT WAS TRY NO. 11
TOO LOW,GUESS AGAIN 327
THAT WAS TRY NO. 12
TOO HIGH,GUESS AGAIN 328


THAT WAS TRY NO. 13
TOO HIGH,GUESS AGAIN 326
THAT WAS TRY NO. 14


YES, YOU GOT IT
 326 IS THE NUMBER
YOU GOT IT
IN 14 TRIES
```

Two Dice

Here's a quick way to add real dice to any fun program you are designing for your computer.

This program rolls two dice and lets you see the results, as with real dice. This is especially useful in those games where it is important to see the value of each.

The subroutine in lines 100-140 generates the necessary pair of random numbers. Lines 60, 70 and 80 make the display you want.

Note that lines 60 and 80 each have nine asterisks. Line 140 is RETURN and must be the last line in the program.

After you type in and RUN the program, press RETURN on your computer's keyboard to roll the dice.

Program Listing

```
10 Q=RND(-TI)
20 PRINT CHR$(147):REM SCREEN CLEAR
30 PRINT"PRESS RETURN"
40 INPUT"TO ROLL TWO DICE";K$:PRINT:PRINT
45 PRINT CHR$(147):REM SCREEN CLEAR
50 GOSUB 100
60 PRINT"*********"
70 PRINT"*";DL;"*";DR;"*"
80 PRINT"*********"
90 PRINT:PRINT:GOTO 30
100 DL=INT(7*RND(1))
110 IF DL<1 THEN 100
120 DR=INT(7*RND(1))
130 IF DR<1 THEN 120
140 RETURN
```

Coin Toss

Here's a handy way to settle arguments. Toss a coin. Only this time, let the computer do the work!

Type in the program. Run it. The computer will report *heads* or *tails* after each toss.

For a new toss, press the RETURN key on your computer's keyboard.

Line 10 clears the screen. A random number—either zero or one—is generated at line 20 and tested to see if it is a zero. If it is, the computer prints *heads*. If not, the computer drops to line 30 where it prints *tails*. Lines 50, 60 and 70 accomplish the restart when you press RETURN.

Program Listing

```
10 PRINT CHR$(147):REM SCREEN CLEAR
15 Q=RND(-TI)
20 IF (INT(2*(RND(1))))<1 THEN PRINT
   "HEADS":GOTO 40
30 PRINT "TAILS"
40 PRINT:PRINT:PRINT
50 PRINT"PRESS RETURN"
60 INPUT"TO TOSS ANOTHER COIN";K$
70 CLR
80 GOTO 10
```

Smart Adder

One of the fun ways to use your computer is in wowing your friends. Next time they ask, "But, what can it do?", show them its uncanny abilities at adding, spelling, writing upside down, even cracking jokes. Try this *Smart Adder* program on your friends. When your neighbors drop in for a cup of coffee, bring out the computer for a demonstration of its lightning speed. You'll love their reactions.

This program adds long strings of numbers in a flash. You give the computer a number. It starts at 1 and adds all numbers up to and including your number. For instance, if you give it a five, it will add 1 plus 2 plus 3 plus 4 plus 5 and display the result.

Ask your neighbor how fast he or she can add all the numbers to 100. It should take several minutes. While he's working on it, let your computer do it in a split second. Your neighbor's reaction is bound to be, "Gee whiz!"

Program Listing

```
10 PRINT CHR$(147)
20 INPUT"GIVE ME A NUMBER";N
30 IF N<1 THEN 20
40 FOR L=1 TO N:X=X+L:NEXT L
50 PRINT:PRINT"THE TOTAL OF"
60 PRINT"ALL NUMBERS"
70 PRINT"FROM 1 TO";N
80 PRINT"IS";X
90 PRINT:PRINT:PRINT:PRINT
100 CLR:GOTO 20
```

Memory Tester

Most everybody can remember numbers. At least short numbers with few digits. But how long a number can you recall in a flash?

The computer will briefly display a number. It then will remove the number from your view and ask you to repeat what it was. If you miss three times, the computer will tell you to FORGET IT, give you your score and end the game. Then it will start over.

On the other hand, if you recall correctly, the computer will say so and then give you a new number. The new number will have more digits than the previous number. Each time you guess correctly, the number gets longer.

No matter how good you are, at some point you won't be able to recall *all* the digits in proper sequence.

How many digits can you quickly recall?

Program Listing

```
10 PRINT CHR$(147):REM CLEAR SCREEN
20 Q=RND(-TI):Z=1
30 S=10*RND(1)
40 N=INT(S*Z)
50 PRINT"REMEMBER---->";N
60 IF W=3 THEN PRINT"FORGET IT !":GOTO 140
70 FOR T=1 TO 1000:NEXT T
80 PRINT CHR$(147):REM SCREEN CLEAR
90 INPUT"WHAT WAS IT";S
100 IF S<>N THEN PRINT"***YOU ARE WRONG***"
    :W=W+1:GOTO 60
110 PRINT"***YOU ARE RIGHT***":R=R+1:Z=Z*10
120 PRINT R;"RIGHT SO FAR"
125 FOR T=1 TO 1000:NEXT T
130 PRINT:GOTO 30
140 PRINT:PRINT"YOU HAD";R;"RIGHT"
150 PRINT:PRINT"LET'S START OVER"
160 PRINT"PRESS ANY KEY"
170 GET K$
180 IF K$="" THEN 170
190 CLR:GOTO 10
```

Super Slot-0

As with all the programs used as examples in this book, simply type this one in and RUN it. The computer will display, on your video screen, the name of this program and some simple instructions.

To simulate pulling the slot machine's lever arm, press the RETURN key on the keyboard.

Program Listing

```
10 PRINT CHR$(147):REM SCREEN CLEAR
20 GOSUB 500
30 PRINT:PRINT:PRINT:PRINT
40 GOSUB 200
50 PRINT" *****  *****  *****"
60 PRINT" * ";A$;" *   * ";B$;" *   * "
   ;C$;" *"
70 PRINT" *****  *****  *****"
80 PRINT:PRINT:PRINT:PRINT
90 PRINT"TO PULL THE LEVER,"
100 INPUT"PRESS RETURN";K$
110 CLR
120 GOTO 10
200 GOSUB 400
210 A$=CHR$(X)
220 GOSUB 400
230 B$=CHR$(X)
240 GOSUB 400
250 C$=CHR$(X)
260 RETURN
400 R=INT(4*RND(1))
410 IF R<1 THEN 400
420 IF R=1 THEN X=97
430 IF R=2 THEN X=115
440 IF R=3 THEN X=122
450 RETURN
500 PRINT" *********************"
510 PRINT" * COMMODORE SLOT-O *"
520 PRINT" *********************"
530 RETURN
```

Three-Digit Mystery

Have your neighbor secretly select any three-digit number in which all three digits are the same. Then have him tell the computer only the *sum* of those three digits. The computer will identify his secret number!

Program Listing

```
10 PRINT CHR$(147)
20 PRINT"SELECT A"
30 PRINT"THREE-DIGIT NUMBER"
40 PRINT"WITH ALL THREE"
50 PRINT"DIGITS THE SAME."
60 PRINT
70 PRINT"ADD THE THREE"
80 PRINT"DIGITS TOGETHER"
90 PRINT
100 PRINT"WHAT IS THE SUM OF"
110 INPUT"THE THREE DIGITS";N
120 IF N<3 OR N>27 THEN 100
130 Q=37*N
140 PRINT:PRINT
150 PRINT"YOUR NUMBER IS";Q
160 FOR L=1 TO 7:PRINT:NEXT L
170 CLR:GOTO 20
```

Yes/No Decision Maker

This is handy for the busy executive who doesn't have time for decisions.

Line 10 clears the screen. Line 20 generates a random number from zero to 100. Line 20 selects a *yes* answer if the random number is greater than 49. Otherwise, line 30 chooses a *no* answer.　　Press any key to repeat the run.

Program Listing

```
10 PRINT CHR$(147):Z=RND(-TI)
20 IF (100*RND(1))>49 THEN PRINT"YES"
   :GOTO 40
30 PRINT"NO"
40 GET K$:IF K$="" THEN 40
50 GOTO 10
```

Executive Decision Maker

Stumped by a toughie? Got one too hot to handle alone? Need help with major decisions? When there is no other way to decide, punch up this quickie and get a definite YES or NO.

Program Listing

```
10 PRINT CHR$(147)
20 Q=RND(-TI)
30 R=INT(1000*RND(1))
40 PRINT:PRINT:PRINT
50 IF R>499 THEN PRINT TAB(8) "YES"
   :GOTO 100
60 PRINT TAB(8) "NO"
100 FOR L=1 TO 12:PRINT:NEXT L
110 PRINT" PRESS ANY KEY"
120 PRINT" TO MAKE ANOTHER"
130 PRINT" IMPORTANT DECISION"
140 GET K$
150 IF K$="" THEN 140
160 CLR
170 GOTO 10
```

Superior Decision Maker

Remember the YES/NO and Executive Decision Makers? Well, the power in the Commodore computer makes an improved decision maker possible.

In this superior edition, a choice of eight replies is possible.

After a run, the computer awaits your press of any key to do another.

Program Listing

```
10 DATA FIRE SOMEONE
20 DATA PASS THE BUCK
30 DATA YES
40 DATA MAYBE
50 DATA REORGANIZE
60 DATA SIT ON IT
70 DATA NO
80 DATA SEE YOUR ANALYST
90 Q=RND(-TI)
100 PRINT CHR$(147)
110 N=INT(9*RND(1))
120 IF N<1 THEN 110
130 FOR L=1 TO N
140 READ Z$
150 NEXT L
160 PRINT Z$
170 GET K$
180 IF K$="" THEN 170
190 RESTORE
200 GOTO 100
```

High/Low Bowling Score

Suppose you bowl with a group of friends, each with a different score or set of scores? This program accepts their names and scores and sorts out the persons with the highest and the lowest bowling scores.

To complete data entry, simply press RETURN without data. That prompts your computer, via lines 120 and 130, to print the lowest score and the highest score.

Naturally, this kind of sorting could be applied to any game with ranges of scores among different players.

Program Listing

```
10 PRINT CHR$(147):REM CLEAR SCREEN
20 INPUT"NAME: ";N$
30 IF N$="" THEN 110
40 INPUT"SCORE: ";S
50 X=X+1
60 IF X=1 THEN LS=S:LN$=N$:HS=S:HN$=N$
70 IF S<LS THEN LS=S:LN$=N$
80 IF S>HS THEN HS=S:HN$=N$
90 N$=""
100 GOTO 20
110 PRINT:PRINT
120 PRINT"LOWEST SCORE:   ",LN$;" ";LS
130 PRINT"HIGHEST SCORE: ",HN$;" ";HS
140 PRINT:PRINT:PRINT
150 PRINT"TO DO MORE,"
160 INPUT"PRESS RETURN";K$
170 CLR
180 GOTO 10
```

Sample Run

```
RUN  RETURN
NAME:
JOHN RETURN
SCORE: 50

NAME:
SUSAN RETURN
SCORE:
89 RETURN
```

```
NAME:
SCOTT   RETURN
SCORE:
72 RETURN

NAME:
BOB RETURN
SCORE:
67 RETURN

NAME:
TOM RETURN
SCORE:
87 RETURN

NAME:
RETURN

LOWEST  SCORE: JOHN 50
HIGHEST SCORE: SUSAN 89
```

Funny similes

Give these newfangled gadgets an inch and they'll take a mile. In the case of the computer, give it some tacky retorts and it will spew out an endless string of dumb remarks.

The fun is in having the computer randomly select various words and combine them to make silly sayings.

The random number is used to match the words into similes.

Program Listing

```
10 PRINT CHR$(147):REM CLEAR SCREEN
20 DATA SHORT,TALL,FAT,LEAN,CLEAN
30 DATA DIRTY,GOOD,BAD,HAPPY,SAD
40 DATA GREEN,RED,YELLOW,BLUE,UGLY
```

```
50 DATA PRETTY,SHARP,DULL,TACKY,NATTY
60 DATA STRONG,WEAK,MEAN,NICE,DUMB
70 DATA GNOME,TREE,PIG,BOX,CLOCK
80 DATA TURKEY,DRAGON,NURD,DOG,ROOKIE
90 DATA BEET,BIRD,SKYHAWK,OAK TREE,PEACH
100 DATA TACK,RAZOR,PIN,PLUG,BULL
110 DATA WORM,LION,LAMB,PUPPY,OX
120 Q=RND(-TI)
200 PRINT"WHOM ARE WE DESCRIBING TODAY"
210 INPUT B$
300 T=INT(26*RND(1))
310 IF T<1 OR T>25 THEN 300
320 FOR L=1 TO T
330 READ D$
340 NEXT L
350 RESTORE
400 T=INT(51*RND(1))
410 IF T<26 OR T>50 THEN 400
420 FOR L=1 TO T
430 READ E$
440 NEXT L
450 RESTORE
500 PRINT CHR$(147)
510 PRINT B$;" IS ";D$
520 PRINT"AS A ";E$
530 PRINT:PRINT:PRINT
600 INPUT"FOR MORE, PRESS RETURN";K$
610 CLR
620 GOTO 10
```

Draw Straws

Here's one of man's oldest decision makers. Several straws are broken off to the same length except for one extra-short straw. The length of all straws is concealed and each person draws a straw. The person drawing the shortest straw "wins." That is, he is selected by the luck of the draw.

Now, your computer can provide a fast and easy drawing where no straws are available. It does all the work for you by assigning electronic straws randomly to each person. Those straws are numbers. The shortest straw, or lowest number, "wins."

Program Listing

```
10 PRINT CHR$(147):REM SCREEN CLEAR
15 Q=RND(-TI)
20 PRINT SPC(5);
30 FOR L=1 TO 11:PRINT CHR$(113);:NEXT L
40 PRINT
50 PRINT SPC(5);"DRAW STRAWS"
60 PRINT SPC(5);
70 FOR L=1 TO 11:PRINT CHR$(113);:NEXT L
80 PRINT:PRINT
90 INPUT"NAME PLAYER 1";B$
100 INPUT"NAME PLAYER 2";C$
110 INPUT"NAME PLAYER 3";D$
120 B=INT(100*(RND(1)))
130 L=B
140 C=INT(100*(RND(1)))
150 IF C<L THEN L=C
160 D=INT(100*(RND(1)))
170 IF D<L THEN L=D
180 PRINT:PRINT
190 IF L=B THEN PRINT CHR$(18);B$,B
    ;CHR$(146):GOTO 210
200 PRINT B$,B
210 IF L=C THEN PRINT CHR$(18);C$,C
    ;CHR$(146):GOTO 230
220 PRINT C$,C
230 IF L=D THEN PRINT CHR$(18);D$,D
    ;CHR$(146):GOTO 250
240 PRINT D$,D
```

```
250 PRINT:PRINT:PRINT
260 INPUT"FOR MORE, PRESS RETURN";K$
270 CLR
280 GOTO 10
```

Learning Programs

Math Flasher

Here's the basic routine (no pun intended) for an educational flash-card program. This one is bare-bones, no frills. You can dress it up with more colorful right-n-wrong messages, opening and closing billboards, etc. You could even make it keep score and present a "batting average" at the end of its run.

Here's how it works:

Lines 10-90 determine which type of math you wish to do. Lines 60-90 move program action to the appropriate group of lines further along in the program.

Lines 200-290 handle addition. Lines 400-490, subtraction. Lines 600-690, multiplication. Lines 800-890, division.

For example, look at lines 200-290. Two separate random numbers are generated (lines 200 and 210). The random numbers are labeled P and Q. At line 230, the program uses P and Q and asks you to add them together. Line 230 waits for and accepts your answer.

At line 260, the program makes the right or wrong decision, using the powerful IF/THEN statement. Line 280 prints the correct answer.

Program execution for subtract (lines 400-490), multiply (lines 600-690), and divide (lines 800-890), are similar except for line 420 in subtraction and line 830 in division.

We make the assumption that it is not desirable to have negative numbers as results of subtraction. That is, we want only subtraction problems with results of zero, one, two, three, or higher. We want no problems which would result in answers below zero such as -1, -2, -3, and so forth. So, line 420 tests P and Q, before presenting the problem on the screen. If they will result in a negative-number answer, then the program returns to lines 400-410 for two new numbers.

In division, we want whole-number answers. That is, we want answers like 2 or 11 or 26. Not answers like 1.81 or 9.75 or 21.3343. So, line 830 tests P and Q to make sure their dividend will be a whole number. If not, the program goes back to line 800 and line 810 for two new numbers.

Program Listing

```
10 PRINT CHR$(147):REM CLEAR SCREEN
20 PRINT"  DO YOU WANT TO"
30 PRINT"ADD","SUBTRACT","MULTIPLY",
   "DIVIDE"
40 PRINT:PRINT
50 GOTO 1020
60 IF LEFT$(K$,1)="A" THEN 200
70 IF LEFT$(K$,1)="S" THEN 400
80 IF LEFT$(K$,1)="M" THEN 600
90 IF LEFT$(K$,1)="D" THEN 800
100 GOTO 40
200 P=INT(10*RND(1))
210 Q=INT(10*RND(1))
220 PRINT
230 PRINT"ADD";P;"PLUS";Q
240 INPUT R
250 PRINT
260 IF R=P+Q THEN PRINT "RIGHT":GOTO 280
270 PRINT"WRONG"
280 PRINT P;"+";Q;"EQUALS";P+Q
290 GOTO 1000
400 P=INT(10*RND(1))
410 Q=INT(10*RND(1))
420 IF P-Q<0 THEN 400
430 PRINT"SUBTRACT";Q;"FROM";P
440 INPUT R
450 PRINT
460 IF R=P-Q THEN PRINT "RIGHT":GOTO 480
470 PRINT"WRONG"
480 PRINT P;"MINUS";Q;"EQUALS";P-Q
490 GOTO 1000
600 P=INT(10*RND(1))
610 Q=INT(10*RND(1))
620 PRINT"MULTIPLY";P;"TIMES";Q
630 INPUT R
640 PRINT
650 IF R=P*Q THEN PRINT "RIGHT":GOTO 670
660 PRINT"WRONG"
670 PRINT P;"TIMES";Q;"EQUALS";P*Q
680 PRINT
```

62

```
690 GOTO 1000
800 P=INT(100*RND(1))
810 Q=INT(10*RND(1))
820 IF Q=0 THEN 800
830 IF (P/Q)<>INT(P/Q) THEN 800
835 PRINT"DIVIDE";P;"BY";Q
840 INPUT R
850 PRINT
860 IF R=P/Q THEN PRINT "RIGHT":GOTO 880
870 PRINT"WRONG"
880 PRINT P;"/";Q;"EQUALS";P/Q
890 PRINT
1000 PRINT:PRINT:PRINT
1010 PRINT"TO DO MORE MATH,"
1020 PRINT"PRESS ONE KEY"
1030 PRINT
1040 PRINT"A(ADD)","S(SUBTRCT)",
     "M(MULTPLY)","D(DIVIDE)","    Q
     (TO QUIT)"
1050 GET K$
1060 IF K$="" THEN 1050
1065 PRINT CHR$(147):REM SCREEN CLEAR
1070 IF K$="Q" THEN 1100
1080 IF K$="A" OR K$="S" OR K$="M" OR
     K$="D" THEN 60
1090 GOTO 1020
1100 PRINT CHR$(147):REM CLEAR SCREEN
1110 PRINT"OKAY, BYE BYE"
1120 END
```

Advanced Math Flasher

Similar to the previous Math Flasher program, this version permits negative numbers and decimal answers.

The range of possible problems has been expanded by using 100*RND(1) in lines 200, 210, 400, 410, 600 and 610, 800, 810 rather than 10*RND(1).

Deleting lines 420 and 830 from the easier Flasher program allows occasional negative numbers to result from subtraction problems and fractional (decimal) numbers to result from division.

Watch out! You may have to resort to the old-fashioned pencil-and-paper method of calculating answers to this program.

Program Listing

```
10 PRINT CHR$(147):REM CLEAR SCREEN
20 PRINT"  DO YOU WANT TO"
30 PRINT"ADD","SUBTRACT","MULTIPLY",
   "DIVIDE"
40 PRINT:PRINT
50 GOTO 1020
60 IF LEFT$(K$,1)="A" THEN 200
70 IF LEFT$(K$,1)="S" THEN 400
80 IF LEFT$(K$,1)="M" THEN 600
90 IF LEFT$(K$,1)="D" THEN 800
100 GOTO 40
200 P=INT(100*RND(1))
210 Q=INT(100*RND(1))
220 PRINT
230 PRINT"ADD";P;"PLUS";Q
240 INPUT R
250 PRINT
260 IF R=P+Q THEN PRINT "RIGHT":GOTO 280
270 PRINT"WRONG"
280 PRINT P;"+";Q;"EQUALS";P+Q
290 GOTO 1000
400 P=INT(100*RND(1))
410 Q=INT(100*RND(1))
430 PRINT"SUBTRACT";Q;"FROM";P
440 INPUT R
450 PRINT
460 IF R=P-Q THEN PRINT "RIGHT":GOTO 480
470 PRINT"WRONG"
480 PRINT P;"MINUS";Q;"EQUALS";P-Q
490 GOTO 1000
600 P=INT(100*RND(1))
610 Q=INT(100*RND(1))
```

64

```
620 PRINT"MULTIPLY";P;"TIMES";Q
630 INPUT R
640 PRINT
650 IF R=P*Q THEN PRINT "RIGHT":GOTO 670
660 PRINT"WRONG"
670 PRINT P;"TIMES";Q;"EQUALS";P*Q
680 PRINT
690 GOTO 1000
800 P=INT(100*RND(1))
810 Q=INT(100*RND(1))
820 IF Q=0 THEN 800
835 PRINT"DIVIDE";P;"BY";Q
840 INPUT R
850 PRINT
860 IF R=P/Q THEN PRINT "RIGHT":GOTO 880
870 PRINT"WRONG"
880 PRINT P;"/";Q;"EQUALS";P/Q
890 PRINT
1000 PRINT:PRINT:PRINT
1010 PRINT"TO DO MORE MATH,"
1020 PRINT"PRESS ONE KEY"
1030 PRINT
1040 PRINT"A(ADD)","S(SUBTRCT)",
     "M(MULTPLY)","D(DIVIDE)","
     Q (TO QUIT)"
1050 GET K$
1060 IF K$="" THEN 1050
1065 PRINT CHR$(147):REM SCREEN CLEAR
1070 IF K$="Q" THEN 1100
1080 IF K$="A" OR K$="S" OR K$="M" OR
     K$="D" THEN 60
1090 GOTO 1020
1100 PRINT CHR$(147):REM CLEAR SCREEN
1110 PRINT"OKAY, BYE BYE"
1120 END
```

U.S. Presidents

Fourteenth. Let's see, that was Franklin Pierce. *Cor-*

rect. *The fourteenth president was Franklin Pierce.* Let's try another. *Thirty-fourth.* John F. Kennedy. *Wrong. The thirty-fourth president was Dwight D. Eisenhower.*

How many of the 40 U.S. presidents can you name? Bet not as many as you would like!

This program tests not only your knowledge of the name of each president and his number in rank, but also the spelling of his name.

The more you take this test, the more you learn.

Program Listing

```
10 PRINT CHR$(147):REM CLEAR SCREEN
20 Q=RND(-TI)
30 DATA FIRST,GEORGE WASHINGTON
40 DATA SECOND,JOHN ADAMS
50 DATA THIRD,THOMAS JEFFERSON
60 DATA FOURTH,JAMES MADISON
70 DATA FIFTH,JAMES MONROE
80 DATA SIXTH,JOHN QUINCY ADAMS
90 DATA SEVENTH,ANDREW JACKSON
100 DATA EIGHTH,MARTIN VAN BUREN
110 DATA NINTH,WILLIAM H. HARRISON
120 DATA TENTH,JOHN TYLER
130 DATA ELEVENTH,JAMES K. POLK
140 DATA TWELFTH,ZACHARY TAYLOR
150 DATA THIRTEENTH,MILLARD FILLMORE
160 DATA FOURTEENTH,FRANKLIN PIERCE
170 DATA FIFTEENTH,JAMES BUCHANAN
180 DATA SIXTEENTH,ABRAHAM LINCOLN
190 DATA SEVENTEENTH,ANDREW JOHNSON
200 DATA EIGHTEENTH,ULYSSES S. GRANT
210 DATA NINTEENTH,RUTHERFORD B. HAYES
220 DATA TWENTIETH,JAMES A. GARFIELD
230 DATA TWENTY-FIRST,CHESTER A. ARTHUR
240 DATA TWENTY-SECOND,GROVER CLEVELAND
250 DATA TWENTY-THIRD,BENJAMIN HARRISON
260 DATA TWENTY-FOURTH,GROVER CLEVELAND
270 DATA TWENTY-FIFTH,WILLIAM MCKINLEY
280 DATA TWENTY-SIXTH,THEODORE ROOSEVELT
290 DATA TWENTY-SEVENTH,WILLIAM H. TAFT
300 DATA TWENTY-EIGHTH,WOODROW WILSON
```

```
310 DATA TWENTY-NINTH,WARREN G. HARDING
320 DATA THIRTIETH,CALVIN COOLIDGE
330 DATA THIRTY-FIRST,HERBERT HOOVER
340 DATA THIRTY-SECOND,FRANKLIN D. ROOSEVELT
350 DATA THIRTY-THIRD,HARRY S TRUMAN
360 DATA THIRTY-FOURTH,DWIGHT D. EISENHOWER
370 DATA THIRTY-FIFTH,JOHN F. KENNEDY
380 DATA THIRTY-SIXTH,LYNDON B. JOHNSON
390 DATA THIRTY-SEVENTH,RICHARD M. NIXON
400 DATA THIRTY-EIGHTH,GERALD R. FORD
410 DATA THIRTY-NINTH,JIMMY CARTER
420 DATA FOURTIETH,RONALD REAGAN
430 PRINT" ********************"
440 PRINT" * U.S. PRESIDENTS *"
450 PRINT" ********************"
460 PRINT
470 PRINT"HOW MANY CAN YOU NAME?"
480 FOR Q=1 TO 11
490 PRINT
500 NEXT Q
510 PRINT"PRESS ANY KEY TO START"
520 GET K$
530 IF K$="" THEN 520
540 PRINT CHR$(147)
550 R=INT(81*RND(1))
560 IF R<1 THEN 550
570 IF INT(R/2)=R/2 THEN R=R-1
600 FOR L=1 TO R
610 READ S$
620 NEXT L
630 PRINT"WHO WAS THE"
640 PRINT S$
650 PRINT"PRESIDENT OF THE"
660 READ C$
670 INPUT"UNITED STATES";D$
680 PRINT:PRINT
700 IF D$=C$ THEN PRINT"CORRECT":GOTO 720
710 PRINT"WRONG"
720 PRINT"THE"
730 PRINT S$
740 PRINT"PRESIDENT WAS"
750 PRINT C$
```

```
760 RESTORE
770 PRINT:PRINT:PRINT
780 PRINT"FOR MORE PRESS M"
790 PRINT"TO QUIT PRESS Q"
800 K$=""
810 GET K$
820 IF K$="" THEN 810
830 IF K$="M" THEN 540
840 IF K$="Q" THEN 900
850 GOTO 770
900 PRINT CHR$(147)
910 PRINT"OKAY, END OF TEST"
920 PRINT"THANK YOU"
```

Sample Run

```
********************
* U.S. PRESIDENTS *
********************
HOW MANY CAN YOU NAME?
PRESS ANY KEY TO START

WHO WAS THE
SEVENTH
PRESIDENT OF THE
UNITED STATES?
ANDREW JACKSON
CORRECT
THE SEVENTH PRESIDENT
WAS ANDREW JACKSON

FOR MORE, PRESS M
TO QUIT,  PRESS Q

WHO WAS THE
THIRTY-THIRD
PRESIDENT OF THE
UNITED STATES?
HARRY S TRUMAN
CORRECT
THE THIRTY-THIRD PRESIDENT
WAS HARRY S TRUMAN
```

```
FOR MORE, PRESS M
TO QUIT, PRESS Q

WHO WAS THE
SIXTH
PRESIDENT OF THE
UNITED STATES?
BARNEY MILLER
WRONG
THE SIXTH PRESIDENT
WAS JOHN QUINCY ADAMS

FOR MORE, PRESS M
TO QUIT, PRESS Q




WHO WAS THE
THIRTY-FOURTH
PRESIDENT OF THE
UNITED STATES?
DWIGHT D. EISENHOWER
CORRECT
THE THIRTY-FOURTH PRESIDENT
WAS DWIGHT D. EISENHOWER

FOR MORE, PRESS M
TO QUIT, PRESS Q




WHO WAS THE
EIGHTH
PRESIDENT OF THE
UNITED STATES?
FRED MERTZ
WRONG
THE EIGHTH PRESIDENT
WAS MARTIN VAN BUREN

FOR MORE, PRESS M
TO QUIT, PRESS Q
```

```
WHO WAS THE
TWENTY-NINTH
PRESIDENT OF THE
UNITED STATES?
WARREN G. HARDING
CORRECT
THE TWENTY-NINTH PRESIDENT
WAS WARREN G. HARDING

FOR MORE, PRESS M
TO QUIT,  PRESS Q
```

State Geographic Centers

This mind bender tests your knowledge of geographic locations of cities and towns in the United States. These are special places since, in each case, they are the town nearest to the geographic center of its state.

In other words, Columbus happens to be almost exactly in the center of Ohio. But which state has Challis at its center? Or Lewistown? Or Oklahoma City? (Well, some may be obvious!)

You not only learn a lot from running this program but you have a barrel of fun. Talk about trivia!

Program Listing

```
10 PRINT CHR$(147)
20 DATA CLANTON,ALABAMA
30 DATA MT. MCKINLEY,ALASKA
40 DATA PRESCOTT,ARIZONA
50 DATA LITTLE ROCK,ARKANSAS
60 DATA MADERA,CALIFORNIA
70 DATA PIKES PEAK,COLORADO
80 DATA EAST BERLIN,CONNECTICUT
90 DATA DOVER,DELAWARE
100 DATA BROOKSVILLE,FLORIDA
110 DATA MACON,GEORGIA
```

```
120 DATA MAUI ISLAND,HAWAII
130 DATA CHALLIS,IDAHO
140 DATA SPRINGFIELD,ILLINOIS
150 DATA INDIANAPOLIS,INDIANA
160 DATA AMES,IOWA
170 DATA GREAT BANK,KANSAS
180 DATA LEBANON,KENTUCKY
190 DATA MARKSVILLE,LOUISIANA
200 DATA DOVER/FOXCROFT,MAINE
210 DATA DAVIDSONVILLE,MARYLAND
220 DATA WORCESTER,MASSACHUSETTS
230 DATA CADILLAC,MICHIGAN
240 DATA BRAINERD,MINNESOTA
250 DATA CARTHAGE,MISSISSIPPI
260 DATA JEFFERSON CITY,MISSOURI
270 DATA LEWISTOWN,MONTANA
280 DATA BROKEN BOW,NEBRASKA
290 DATA AUSTIN,NEVADA
300 DATA ASHLAND,NEW HAMPSHIRE
310 DATA TRENTON,NEW JERSEY
320 DATA WILLARD,NEW MEXICO
330 DATA ONEIDA,NEW YORK
340 DATA SANFORD,NORTH CAROLINA
350 DATA MCCLUSKY,NORTH DAKOTA
360 DATA COLUMBUS,OHIO
370 DATA OKLAHOMA CITY,OKLAHOMA
380 DATA PRINEVILLE,OREGON
390 DATA BELLEFONTE,PENNSYLVANIA
400 DATA CROMPTON,RHODE ISLAND
410 DATA COLUMBIA,SOUTH CAROLINA
420 DATA PIERRE,SOUTH DAKOTA
430 DATA MURFREESBORO,TENNESSEE
440 DATA BRADY,TEXAS
450 DATA MANTI,UTAH
460 DATA ROXBURY,VERMONT
470 DATA BUCKINGHAM,VIRGINIA
480 DATA WENATCHEE,WASHINGTON
490 DATA SUTTON,WEST VIRGINIA
500 DATA MARSHFIELD,WISCONSIN
510 DATA LANDER,WYOMING
520 PRINT"FOR HOW MANY STATES"
530 PRINT"CAN YOU NAME THE"
```

```
540 PRINT"GEOGRAPHICAL CENTER?"
550 Q=RND(-TI)
560 R=INT(100*RND(1))
570 IF R<1 THEN 560
580 IF INT(R/2)=R/2 THEN R=R-1
590 FOR L=1 TO R
600 READ S$
610 NEXT L
620 PRINT:PRINT:PRINT
630 PRINT"WHICH STATE HAS ITS"
640 PRINT"GEOGRAPHIC CENTER NEAR"
650 PRINT S$
660 READ C$
670 INPUT D$
675 PRINT CHR$(147)
680 PRINT
690 IF C$=D$ THEN PRINT"CORRECT":GOTO 710
700 PRINT"WRONG"
710 PRINT
720 PRINT S$;" IS"
730 PRINT"THE CENTER OF"
740 PRINT C$
750 RESTORE
760 PRINT:PRINT:PRINT
770 GOTO 560
```

Sample Run

```
FOR HOW MANY STATES
CAN YOU NAME THE
GEOGRAPHICAL CENTER?

WHICH STATE HAS ITS
GEOGRAPHIC CENTER NEAR
DOVER?  DELAWARE
CORRECT

DOVER IS
THE CENTER OF
DELAWARE
```

```
WHICH STATE HAS ITS
GEOGRAPHICAL CENTER NEAR
COLUMBUS? GEORGIA

WRONG
COLUMBUS IS
THE CENTER OF
OHIO
```

Foreign Capitals

Here's a learning quiz we'll bet you haven't seen anywhere else. This program tests your knowledge of foreign countries. The more you play, the more you learn!

You must tell the computer the correct name of the capital of the country it presents. And you must spell the name of that city correctly.

What is the capital of Egypt, Poland, Turkey, New Zealand, Bolivia or Afghanistan? It can be very tough!

Want to change to different countries? Change the DATA lines 20 to 540. Be sure to put a comma between country and capital in each DATA line.

Program Listing

```
10 PRINT CHR$(147):REM CLEAR SCREEN
15 Q=RND(-TI)
20 DATA AFGHANISTAN,KABUL
30 DATA ALBANIA,TIRANA
40 DATA ALGERIA,ALGIERS
50 DATA ARGENTINA,BUENOS AIRES
60 DATA AUSTRALIA,CANBERRA
70 DATA AUSTRIA,VIENNA
80 DATA BAHRAIN,MANAMA
90 DATA BANGLADESH,DACCA
100 DATA BELGIUM,BRUSSELS
110 DATA BOLIVIA,LA PAZ
120 DATA BRAZIL,BRASILIA
```

```
130 DATA BULGARIA,SOFIA
140 DATA BURMA,RANGOON
150 DATA CHILE,SANTIAGO
160 DATA COLOMBIA,BOGOTA
170 DATA CUBA,HAVANA
180 DATA CZECHOSLOVAKIA,PRAGUE
190 DATA DENMARK,COPENHAGEN
200 DATA EAST GERMANY,EAST BERLIN
210 DATA EGYPT,CAIRO
220 DATA FINLAND,HELSINKI
230 DATA FRANCE,PARIS
240 DATA GREECE,ATHENS
250 DATA HAITI,PORT-AU-PRINCE
260 DATA HUNGARY,BUDAPEST
270 DATA ICELAND,REYKJAVIK
280 DATA INDIA,NEW DELHI
290 DATA IRAN,TEHRAN
300 DATA ITALY,ROME
310 DATA JAPAN,TOKYO
320 DATA KUWAIT,KUWAIT
330 DATA LIBYA,TRIPOLI
340 DATA MEXICO,MEXICO CITY
350 DATA NEPAL,KATHMANDU
360 DATA NEW ZEALAND,WELLINGTON
370 DATA NORWAY,OSLO
380 DATA OMAN,MUSCAT
390 DATA PERU,LIMA
400 DATA POLAND,WARSAW
410 DATA QATAR,DOHA
420 DATA ROMANIA,BUCHAREST
430 DATA SPAIN,MADRID
440 DATA SUDAN,KHARTOUM
450 DATA SWEDEN,STOCKHOLM
460 DATA SWITZERLAND,BERN
470 DATA TURKEY,ANKARA
480 DATA U.S.S.R.,MOSCOW
490 DATA UNITED KINGDOM,LONDON
500 DATA VENEZUELA,CARACAS
510 DATA WEST GERMANY,BONN
520 DATA YUGOSLAVIA,BELGRADE
530 DATA ZAIRE,KINSHASA
540 DATA ZAMBIA,LUSAKA
```

```
550 PRINT"**FOREIGN CAPITALS**"
560 PRINT:PRINT"HOW MANY CAN YOU NAME"
570 R=INT(106*(RND(1)))
580 IF R<1 THEN 570
590 IF INT(R/2)=(R/2) THEN R=R-1
600 FOR L=1 TO R
610 READ S$
620 NEXT L
630 PRINT:PRINT
640 PRINT"COUNTRY:"
645 PRINT S$
650 READ C$
655 PRINT
660 PRINT"WHAT IS THE CAPITAL "
665 INPUT D$
670 IF D$=C$ THEN PRINT:PRINT "RIGHT"
    :GOTO 690
680 PRINT:PRINT"WRONG"
690 PRINT"CAPITAL OF ";S$
700 PRINT"IS ";C$
710 RESTORE
720 PRINT:PRINT:PRINT
730 GOTO 570
```

Birthstones

What's your Mother's birthstone? You'd better know!
If not, take this little quiz a few times until you get all 12
months memorized.

The computer presents the name of a month. You
type in the name of the birthstone (correctly spelled) for
that month.

Program Listing

```
10 PRINT CHR$(147):REM CLEAR SCREEN
15 Q=RND(-TI)
20 DATA JANUARY,GARNET
30 DATA FEBRUARY,AMETHYST
```

```
40 DATA MARCH,AQUAMARINE
50 DATA APRIL,DIAMOND
60 DATA MAY,EMERALD
70 DATA JUNE,PEARL
80 DATA JULY,RUBY
90 DATA AUGUST,PERIDOT
100 DATA SEPTEMBER,SAPPHIRE
110 DATA OCTOBER,OPAL
120 DATA NOVEMBER,TOPAZ
130 DATA DECEMBER,TURQUOISE
140 PRINT"    **************"
150 PRINT"    * BIRTHSTONES *"
160 PRINT"    **************"
170 PRINT:PRINT:PRINT
180 PRINT"HOW MANY MONTHS"
190 PRINT"DO YOU KNOW?"
200 PRINT:PRINT
210 PRINT"PRESS ANY KEY TO START"
220 GET K$
230 IF K$="" THEN 220
240 PRINT CHR$(147):REM SCREEN CLEAR
250 R=INT(25*RND(1))
260 IF R<1 THEN 250
270 IF INT(R/2)=(R/2) THEN R=R-1
280 FOR L=1 TO R
290 READ S$
300 NEXT L
310 PRINT"WHAT IS THE"
320 PRINT"BIRTHSTONE FOR"
330 PRINT S$
340 PRINT
350 READ C$
360 INPUT D$
365 PRINT
370 IF D$=C$ THEN PRINT "RIGHT!":GOTO 400
380 PRINT"WRONG!"
400 PRINT"THE BIRTHSTONE"
410 PRINT"FOR ";S$
420 PRINT"IS ";C$
430 RESTORE
440 FOR B=1 TO 6
450 PRINT
```

```
460 NEXT B
470 CLR
480 GOTO 250
```

Sample Run

```
***************
*  BIRTHSTONES  *
***************

HOW MANY MONTHS DO YOU KNOW?
PRESS ANY KEY TO START
WHAT IS THE BIRTHSTONE
FOR JULY?
RUBY
RIGHT !
THE BIRTHSTONE FOR JULY
IS THE RUBY

WHAT IS THE BIRTHSTONE
FOR MAY?
EMERALD
RIGHT !
THE BIRTHSTONE FOR MAY
IS THE EMERALD
```

Number Of Days In A Month

Here's a cute teacher for your elementary-age kids. This program displays the name of a month and asks how many days in that month. If the correct number of days is entered, the computer says "correct." If an incorrect number of days is entered, the computer says "wrong." In either case, the correct answer is displayed. The educational game can go on forever if needed.

Program Listing

```
10 PRINT CHR$(147):REM SCREEN CLEAR
20 DATA JANUARY,31
```

```
30 DATA FEBRUARY,28
40 DATA MARCH,31
50 DATA APRIL,30
60 DATA MAY,31
70 DATA JUNE,30
80 DATA JULY,31
90 DATA AUGUST,31
100 DATA SEPTEMBER,30
110 DATA OCTOBER,31
120 DATA NOVEMBER,30
130 DATA DECEMBER,31
140 Q=RND(-TI)
150 R=INT(25*RND(1))
160 IF R<1 THEN 150
170 IF INT(R/2)=(R/2) THEN R=R-1
180 FOR L=1 TO R
190 READ S$
200 NEXT L
210 PRINT"MONTH IS ";S$
220 READ C$
230 PRINT"HOW MANY DAYS IN ";S$
240 INPUT D$
250 IF D$=C$ THEN PRINT"CORRECT":GOTO 300
260 PRINT"WRONG"
300 PRINT S$;" HAS ";C$;" DAYS"
310 RESTORE
320 PRINT
330 PRINT
340 PRINT
350 GOTO 150
```

Math Helper Programs

Volumes

Cones. Cubes. Cylinders. Prisms. Pyramids. Spheres. Name your object. This program computes the volume and displays it in cubic units.

Put in inches, get cubic inches. Put in feet, get cubic feet. Yards, get cubic yards. No mixing units in any one calculation. Cylinder is right circular.

Program Listing

```
10 GOSUB 900
20 PRINT:PRINT:PRINT
30 INPUT"OBJECT NAME";X$
50 PRINT
60 IF X$="CONE" THEN 100
65 IF X$="PYRAMID" THEN 100
70 IF X$="CUBE" THEN 200
75 IF X$="CYLINDER" THEN 300
80 IF X$="PRISM" THEN 400
85 IF X$="SPHERE" THEN 500
90 PRINT"TRY AGAIN"
95 GOTO 20
100 PRINT X$;" AREA";
110 INPUT A
120 PRINT X$;" HEIGHTH";
130 INPUT H
140 V=(A*H)/3
150 GOTO 600
200 PRINT X$;" LENGTH";
210 INPUT L
220 PRINT X$;" WIDTH";
230 INPUT W
240 PRINT X$;" HEIGHTH";
250 INPUT H
260 V=L*W*H
270 GOTO 600
300 PRINT X$;" RADIUS";
310 INPUT R
320 PRINT X$;" HEIGHTH";
330 INPUT H
```

```
340 V=3.141592654*2*R*H
350 GOTO 600
400 PRINT X$;" AREA";
410 INPUT A
420 PRINT X$;" HEIGHTH";
430 INPUT H
440 V=A*H
450 GOTO 600
500 PRINT X$;" RADIUS";
510 INPUT R
520 V=(3.141592654*4*(R↑3))/3
600 PRINT
610 PRINT X$;" VOLUME ";V
630 GOTO 20
900 PRINT CHR$(147);CHR$(28)
910 PRINT TAB(5);CHR$(111);
920 FOR L=1 TO 11:PRINT CHR$(163);:NEXT L
930 PRINT CHR$(112)
935 PRINT TAB(5);CHR$(165);
940 PRINT TAB(8);"VOLUMES";
950 PRINT TAB(17);CHR$(167)
955 PRINT TAB(5);CHR$(108);
957 FOR L=1 TO 11:PRINT CHR$(164);:NEXT L
960 PRINT TAB(17);CHR$(186)
970 PRINT CHR$(144)
980 RETURN
```

Sample Run

```
OBJECT NAME?      SPHERE
SPHERE RADIUS?    8
SPHERE VOLUME     2144.66058

OBJECT NAME?      PRISM
PRISM AREA?       71
PRISM HEIGHTH?    18
PRISM VOLUME      1278

OBJECT NAME?      CUBE
CUBE LENGTH?      13
CUBE WIDTH?       8
CUBE HEIGHTH?     24
CUBE VOLUME       2496
```

```
OBJECT NAME?       CONE
CONE AREA?         55
CONE HEIGHT?       66
CONE VOLUME        1210

OBJECT NAME?       CYLINDER
CYLINDER RADIUS?   88
CYLINDER HEIGHT?33
CYLINDER VOLUME    18246.3701

OBJECT NAME?       PYRAMID
PYRAMID AREA?      321
PYRAMID HEIGHT?22
PYRAMID VOLUME     2354
```

Areas

Circle. Ellipse. Parabola. Sphere. Square. Rectangle. Triangle. Name your shape. This program will compute its area. Surface area in the case of the sphere. Answer the computer's questions and it will give you the answer you need, in square units of measure. If you use inches, the answer will be in square inches. Put in yards and get square yards. Meters, get square meters. Please don't mix units in any one computation.

Program Listing

```
10 PRINT CHR$(147):REM CLEAR SCREEN
20 INPUT"SHAPE";S$
30 PRINT
40 IF S$="CIRCLE" THEN 200
50 IF S$="ELLIPSE" THEN 300
60 IF S$="PARABOLA" THEN 400
70 IF S$="SPHERE" THEN 500
80 IF S$="SQUARE" THEN 600
90 IF S$="RECTANGLE" THEN 600
100 IF S$="TRIANGLE" THEN 700
```

```
110 PRINT"NOT A RECOGNIZED SHAPE TRY AGAIN"
120 PRINT
130 GOTO 20
200 INPUT"RADIUS";R
210 A=3.141592654*(R↑2)
220 GOTO 800
300 INPUT"MAJOR AXIS";J
310 INPUT"MINOR AXIS";N
320 A=0.7854*J*N
330 GOTO 800
400 INPUT"BASE";B
410 INPUT"HEIGHTH";H
420 A=(2/3)*(B*H)
430 GOTO 800
500 INPUT"RADIUS";R
510 A=3.141592654*4*(R↑2)
520 GOTO 800
600 INPUT"LENGTH";L
610 IF S$="SQUARE" THEN A=L*L:GOTO 800
620 INPUT"WIDTH";W
630 A=L*W
640 GOTO 800
700 INPUT"BASE";B
710 INPUT"HEIGHTH";H
720 A=0.5*B*H
800 PRINT
810 PRINT"AREA ";A
820 PRINT
830 GOTO 20
```

Sample Run

```
SHAPE    TRIANGLE
BASE     55
HEIGHTH    22

AREA   - 605


SHAPE    ELLIPSE
MAJOR AXIS    19
```

```
MINOR AXIS     14

AREA      208.9164
SHAPE     CIRCLE
RADIUS       13

AREA      530.929159

SHAPE     PARABOLA
BASE      18
HEIGHTH      37

AREA      444

SHAPE     SQUARE
LENGTH       44

AREA      1936

SHAPE     SPHERE
RADIUS       13

AREA      2123.71664

SHAPE     RECTANGLE
LENGTH       22
WIDTH        55

AREA      1210
```

Reciprocals

Key in any number. The computer will display its reciprocal. The actual conversion is done here at line 30.

Program Listing

```
10 PRINT CHR$(147):REM CLEAR SCREEN
```

```
15 PRINT"NUMBER TO BE CONVERTED"
20 INPUT"TO ITS RECIPROCAL";N
25 IF N=0 THEN PRINT:GOTO 15
30 R=1/N
40 PRINT:PRINT:PRINT
50 PRINT"RECIPROCAL OF";N
60 PRINT"IS";R
70 PRINT:PRINT:PRINT
80 INPUT"FOR MORE PRESS RETURN";K$
90 CLR:GOTO 10
```

Averages

Key in numbers in any order. A zero will end entry. The computer will tell you the average number of all numbers you entered.

Line 40 finds the total number of all numbers entered. Line 50 finds the total of entered numbers. Line 70 computes the average.

Program Listing

```
10 PRINT CHR$(147):REM CLEAR SCREEN
20 INPUT"GIVE ME A NUMBER";Z
30 IF Z=0 THEN 70
40 N=N+1
50 T=T+Z
60 GOTO 20
70 A=T/N
100 PRINT:PRINT:PRINT
110 PRINT"THE AVERAGE IS";A
120 PRINT:PRINT:PRINT
130 INPUT"FOR MORE PRESS RETURN";K$
140 CLR:GOTO 10
```

Fractional feet

You are measuring a box and the computation comes out to 14.5 feet. How do you change 14.5 feet into 14 feet 6 inches? Here's how:

Program Listing

```
10 PRINT CHR$(147)
20 PRINT"TYPE FRACTIONAL FEET"
30 PRINT"(FEET TO A DECIMAL)"
40 INPUT F
45 W=INT(F)
50 B=F-W
60 D=12*B
62 IF (D-INT(D))<0.5 THEN I=INT(D):GOTO 80
70 I=INT(D)+1
80 PRINT
90 PRINT F;"FEET ="
100 PRINT W;"FEET";I;"INCHES"
200 FOR L=1 TO 10:PRINT:NEXT L
210 INPUT"PRESS RETURN FOR MORE";K$
220 CLR:GOTO 10
```

Sample Run

```
TYPE FRACTIONAL FEET
(FEET TO A DECIMAL)

 14.5 FEET =
 14 FEET 6 INCHES

PRESS RETURN FOR MORE


TYPE FRACTIONAL FEET
(FEET TO A DECIMAL)

 19.8 FEET =
 19 FEET 10 INCHES

PRESS RETURN FOR MORE
```

87

TYPE FRACTIONAL FEET
(FEET TO A DECIMAL)

16.2 FEET =
16 FEET 2 INCHES

PRESS RETURN FOR MORE

TYPE FRACTIONAL FEET
(FEET TO A DECIMAL)

99.7 FEET =
99 FEET 8 INCHES

PRESS RETURN FOR MORE

TYPE FRACTIONAL FEET
(FEET TO A DECIMAL)

32.75 FEET =
32 FEET 9 INCHES

PRESS RETURN FOR MORE

TYPE FRACTIONAL FEET
(FEET TO A DECIMAL)

48 FEET =
48 FEET 0 INCHES

PRESS RETURN FOR MORE

TYPE FRACTIONAL FEET
(FEET TO A DECIMAL)

61.4 FEET =
61 FEET 5 INCHES

PRESS RETURN FOR MORE

Standard Deviation

Here's a way to determine mean and standard deviation. In this particular program, you exit the entry cycle by entering the large number 999999999 (nine 9's) so you can't use 999999999 as one of your data points.

This is a great opportunity to experiment with standard deviation computations. Try a series of data points such as 3, 5, 3, 7, and 4. They should result in

```
DATA POINTS TOTAL 22
MEAN 4.4
VARIANCE 2.23999998
STD DEVIATION 1.49666295
```

Program Listing

```
10 PRINT CHR$(147):REM CLEAR SCREEN
20 INPUT"DATA POINT:";X
30 IF X=999999999 THEN 60
40 T=T+X:S=S+X↑2:N=N+1
50 GOTO 20
60 A=T/N:V=S/N-A↑2:D=SQR(V)
70 PRINT:PRINT:PRINT
80 PRINT"DATA POINTS TOTAL";T
90 PRINT"MEAN";A
100 PRINT"VARIANCE";V
110 PRINT"STD DEVIATION";D
120 PRINT:PRINT:PRINT
130 INPUT"FOR MORE PRESS RETURN";K$
140 CLR:GOTO 10
```

Sample Run

```
DATA POINT: 9
DATA POINT: 8
DATA POINT: 7
DATA POINT: 6
DATA POINT: 5
DATA POINT: 4
DATA POINT: 3
DATA POINT: 2
DATA POINT: 999999999
```

```
DATA POINTS TOTAL 44
MEAN 5.5
VARIANCE 5.25
STD DEVIATION 2.29128785


FOR MORE PRESS RETURN
```

Astronomy
Lightyears/Distance Conversions

Starlight,
Starbright,
I wish I may,
I wish I might,
Know the distance
To your light.

For students of astronomy everywhere, here's how to plug your computer into your hobby: use the machine to discover distances across the Universe!

This program converts lightyears to kilometers or kilometers to lightyears or lightyears to miles or miles to lightyears. It's hard to visualize distances in lightyears. Run this program and you'll be better able to grasp the vast expanse of the Cosmos with your mind.

Of course, all distances are approximate. We use 365.86 days per year and, thus, 9.4830912×10^{12}km/ly or $5.892792872 \times 10^{12}$mi/ly.

Program Listing

```
10 GOSUB 900
20 PRINT:PRINT
```

```
30 PRINT"YOUR CHOICES ARE:"
35 PRINT
40 PRINT"(1) LTYRS TO KILOMTRS"
50 PRINT"(2) LTYRS TO MILES"
60 PRINT"(3) KILOMTRS TO LTYRS"
70 PRINT"(4) MILES TO LTYRS"
80 PRINT
90 PRINT"WHICH CONVERSION?"
100 PRINT"PRESS A NUMBER"
110 GET K$
120 IF K$="" THEN 110
130 IF VAL(K$)<1 OR VAL(K$)>4 THEN 20
140 IF VAL(K$)>2 THEN 400
200 PRINT CHR$(147):REM CLEAR SCREEN
210 INPUT"LIGHTYEARS";L
220 K=L*(9.4630912*(10↑12))
230 M=L*(5.89279287*(10↑12))
240 IF VAL(K$)=2 THEN 300
250 PRINT
260 PRINT K;"KM"
270 PRINT:PRINT:PRINT
280 INPUT"PRESS RETURN FOR MORE";K$
290 CLR:GOTO 10
300 PRINT
310 PRINT M;"MILES"
320 GOTO 270
400 PRINT CHR$(147)
410 IF VAL(K$)=4 THEN 500
420 INPUT"KILOMTRS";K
430 L=K/(9.4630912*(10↑12))
440 PRINT
450 PRINT L;"LTYRS"
460 GOTO 270
500 INPUT"MILES";M
510 L=M/(5.89279287*(10↑12))
520 GOTO 440
890 END
900 PRINT CHR$(147):REM CLEAR SCREEN
910 FOR L=1 TO 22:PRINT CHR$(120);:NEXT L
920 PRINT" LIGHTYEARS  DISTANCE"
930 FOR L=1 TO 22:PRINT CHR$(120);:NEXT L
940 RETURN
```

Photography: Flash Exposure

Use your computer to help take better pictures!

The most important factor in pictures shot with flash is the distance from your flash to the subject. Subjects which are close to you will receive a lot of light while subjects farther away will receive less light.

Check your data sheet for the film you are using. Look for the film guide number. Next, make an estimate of the distance in feet from the flash to your subject.

This program determines the proper f/stop setting for your camera. By the way, if the computer tells you to use an f/stop setting between two f/numbers available on your camera, set your lens opening at the nearest f/number or halfway between the two, whichever is closest.

For example, suppose your film has a guide number of 80 and you estimate the flash-to-subject distance at 10 feet. Use f/8 on your lens.

Program Listing

```
10 PRINT CHR$(147)
20 PRINT"      PHOTOGRAPHY"
30 PRINT"    FLASH EXPOSURE"
40 FOR L=1 TO 22:PRINT CHR$(113);:NEXT L
50 PRINT:PRINT"FILM GUIDE NUMBER"
60 INPUT G
70 IF G=0 THEN 50
80 PRINT"FLASH-TO-SUBJECT"
90 INPUT"DISTANCE";D
100 IF D=0 THEN 80
110 F=G/D
120 PRINT:PRINT"SHOOT AT F/";F
130 FOR L=1 TO 6:PRINT:NEXT L
140 PRINT"TO DO ANOTHER,"
150 INPUT"PRESS RETURN";K$
160 CLR
170 GOTO 10
```

Sample Run

```
        PHOTOGRAPHY
    FLASH EXPOSURE

FILM GUIDE NUMBER
?  80
FLASH-TO-SUBJECT
DISTANCE?  10

SHOOT AT F/8
TO DO ANOTHER,
PRESS RETURN
```

Photography: Close Ups

For copying and other close-up work with your camera, you extend the camera lens by using bellows or extension tubes. In doing that, you must allow for an effective increase in the normal f/number or your picture will be underexposed.

You make such an exposure compensation whenever the subject distance is less than eight times the focal length of your lens.

This program provides a convenient means of determining the effective f/number. For example, if the focal length of your camera is 50mm and the lens-to-film distance (focal length plus extension from infinity position) is 100mm, and the normal f/stop would be 22, the corrected stop would be f/11.

Or, if you are using a 25mm lens, with 50mm lens-to-film distance, a normal f/stop of 8 should be corrected to f/4. Be sure to keep both focal length and distance in either mm or inches. Don't mix apples and oranges.

Program Listing

```
10 PRINT CHR$(147):REM CLEAR SCREEN
20 PRINT"      PHOTOGRAPHY"
30 PRINT"       CLOSE UPS"
```

```
40 FOR L=1 TO 22:PRINT CHR$(97);:NEXT L
50 PRINT:PRINT"WHAT IS THE"
60 INPUT"NORMAL F/NUMBER";F
70 PRINT"LENS-TO-FILM"
80 INPUT"DISTANCE IN MM";D
90 IF D=0 THEN 80
100 PRINT"LENS FOCAL LENGTH"
110 INPUT"IN MM";L
120 N=F*L/D
130 PRINT:PRINT"EFFECTIVE F/NUMBER"
140 PRINT"IS F/";N
150 FOR L=1 TO 6:PRINT:NEXT L
160 PRINT"TO DO MORE,"
170 INPUT"PRESS RETURN";K$
180 CLR
190 GOTO 10
```

Sample Run

```
        PHOTOGRAPHY
          CLOSE UPS
WHAT IS THE
NORMAL F/NUMBER?   22
LENS-TO-FILM
DISTANCE IN MM?    100
LENS FOCAL LENGTH
IN MM?             50

EFFECTIVE F/NUMBER
IS                 F/11

TO DO MORE,
PRESS RETURN
```

Computer books
from ARCsoft Publishers
At Your Bookstore

For the TIMEX/Sinclair 1000, Sinclair ZX-81 and MicroAce:
Practical TIMEX/Sinclair Computer Programs for Beginners
Edward Page $7.95   ISBN 0-86668-027-6
101 TIMEX 1000/Sinclair ZX-81 Programming Tips & Tricks
Edward Page $7.95   ISBN 0-86668-020-9
TIMEX/Sinclair Computer Games Programs
Edward Page $7.95   ISBN 0-86668-026-8
37 TIMEX 1000/Sinclair ZX-81 Programs for Home, School & Office
Edward Page $8.95   ISBN 0-86668-021-7
TIMEX/Sinclair Computer Program Writing Workbook
Edward Page $4.95   ISBN 0-86668-810-2

For the Texas Instruments TI-99/4A Home Computer:
Texas Instruments Home Computer Games Programs
Len Turner $8.95   ISBN 0-86668-032-2
Texas Instruments Home Computer Graphics Programs
Len Turner $9.95   ISBN 0-86668-031-4
101 Programming Tips & Tricks for the Texas Instruments TI-99/4A
Len Turner $8.95   ISBN 0-86668-025-X
36 Texas Instruments TI-99/4A Programs for Home, School & Office
Len Turner $8.95   ISBN 0-86668-024-1
Texas Instruments Computer Program Writing Workbook
Len Turner $4.95   ISBN 0-86668-812-9

For the VIC-20 and Commodore computers:
Commodore 64 Computer Programs for Beginners
Howard Adler $8.95   ISBN 0-86668-033-0
101 Programming Tips & Tricks for the VIC-20 and Commodore 64
Howard Adler $8.95   ISBN 0-86668-030-6
34 VIC-20 Computer Programs for Home, School & Office
Howard Adler $8.95   ISBN 0-86668-029-2
VIC-20 Computer Program Writing Workbook
Howard Adler $4.95   ISBN 0-86668-811-0

For the ATARI computers:
101 ATARI Computer Programming Tips & Tricks
Alan North $8.95   ISBN 0-86668-022-5
31 New ATARI Computer Programs for Home, School & Office
Alan North $8.95   ISBN 0-86668-018-7
ATARI Computer Program Writing Workbook
Alan North $4.95   ISBN 0-86668-814-5

For the TRS-80 Color Computer and TDP-100 computers:
Color Computer Graphics
Ron Clark $9.95   ISBN 0-86668-012-8
101 Color Computer Programming Tips & Tricks
Ron Clark $7.95   ISBN 0-86668-007-1

55 Color Computer Programs for Home School & Office
Ron Clark $9.95 ISBN 0-86668-005-5

55 MORE Color Computer Programs for Home, School & Office
Ron Clark $9.95 ISBN 0-86668-008-X

The Color Computer Songbook
Ron Clark $7.95 ISBN 0-86668-011-X

TRS-80 Color Computer Program Writing Workbook
Ron Clark $4.95 ISBN 0-86668-816-1

My Buttons Are Blue and Other Love Poems
Edited by Ron Clark $4.95 ISBN 0-86668-013-6

For the APPLE and Franklin ACE computers:
101 APPLE Computer Programming Tips & Tricks
Fred White $8.95 ISBN 0-86668-015-2

33 New APPLE Computer Programs for Home, School & Office
Fred White $8.95 ISBN 0-86668-016-0

APPLE Computer Program Writing Workbook
Fred White $4.95 ISBN 0-86668-813-7

For the TRS-80, Sharp and Casio Pocket Computers:
44 Programs for the TRS-80 Model 100 Portable Computer
Jim Cole $8.95 ISBN 0-86668-034-9

Practical PC-2/PC-1500 Pocket Computer Programs
Jim Cole $7.95 ISBN 0-86668-028-4

Pocket Computer Programming Made Easy
Jim Cole $8.95 ISBN 0-86668-009-8

99 Tips & Tricks for the New Pocket Computers
Jim Cole $7.95 ISBN 0-86668-019-5

101 Pocket Computer Programming Tips & Tricks
Jim Cole $7.95 ISBN 0-86668-004-7

Murder In The Mansion and Other Computer Adventures—2nd Edition
Jim Cole $6.95 ISBN 0-86668-501-4

50 Programs in BASIC for Home, School & Office—2nd Edition
Jim Cole $9.95 ISBN 0-86668-502-2

50 MORE Programs in BASIC for Home, School & Office
Jim Cole $9.95 ISBN 0-86668-003-9

Pocket Computer Program Writing Workbook
Jim Cole $4.95 ISBN 0-86668-817-X

35 Practical Programs for the CASIO Pocket Computer
Jim Cole $8.95 ISBN 0-86668-014-4

For the TRS-80 Model I and Model III computers:
TRS-80 Model I/III Computer Program Writing Workbook
Mark Lewis $4.95 ISBN 0-86668-815-3

For the IBM Personal Computer:
IBM Personal Computer Program Writing Workbook
George Bridges $4.95 ISBN 0-86668-818-8

Universal for use with any computer system:
Universal BASIC Computer Program Writing Workbook
Don Roberts $4.95 ISBN 0-86668-819-6

ISBN: International Standard Book Number